7-27-23

Thank you for believing in the power of *Leading Clarity*.

bdeutser@deutser.com | 713.850.2105
DEUTSER.COM | BRADDEUTSER.COM

"Building a purpose means first getting crystal clear on the foundation of your business. It sounds easy but it can elude many, restricting growth and potential. Brad masterfully guides leaders to understand who they are at their core so they can set a course for where they're going."

Carol Cone, founder of The Purpose Collaborative and Cone, Inc.

"I am a true disciple of the principles in *Leading Clarity*. Brad's distinctive ability to distill the most complex, forward-thinking business concepts has changed how I lead. His coaching and insight have helped so many change their business and life."

Jason Siegel, Managing Director, Head of Alternative Investments, Brookfield Asset Management

"Leaders now face unprecedented challenge and opportunity. Strategy is not enough. *Leading Clarity* offers leaders a practical and visionary approach to leading through a landscape of change, chaos, and uncertainty by harnessing and aligning the full potential of their employees. I've long talked about the benefits of collaboration and co-creation and Deutser offers a blueprint for connected engagement at every level of an organization."

Lee E. Miller, author of *A Woman's Guide to Successful Negotiating*

"For all the idea monkeys out there, especially me, this is going to become your new go-to handbook! *Leading Clarity* spotlights how distraction can become the Achilles heel of a company and how integral alignment with every touchpoint is to success. I ate up every page and heard myself saying "Why haven't I thought about that?" out loud while reading. From the anecdotes to the practical exercises, you come away with a solid roadmap and defined steps to ensure you are the confident conductor on the clarity train. This book is what every business owner, leader, and visionary needs to read, practice, and implement so they don't end up on the completely wrong track. I would have saved so much money, time, and sanity if I had this book before I started my business—but it's never too late to redirect."

Mareya Ibrahim, founder and CEO, Grow Green Industries

"Deutser masterfully explores the dynamic interconnectedness that creates organizational clarity. This wonderful book offers leaders at every level practical exercises for accessing and amplifying the power of people to yield greater results."

Neil Bush, Chairman, Barbara Bush Houston Literacy Foundation and Chairman, Points of Light

"Each chapter in this innovative book unfolds to reveal a fresh understanding of the many factors that come together to create a dynamic whole. Deutser delivers a process that simply is brilliant, illustrated by compelling stories and examples from the broad expanse of his experience."

Jeff DeGraff, innovation expert, bestselling author, Professor of Management Education, University of Michigan Ross School of Business

LEADING

CLARITY

The Breakthrough Strategy to Unleash
PEOPLE, PROFIT, and PERFORMANCE

■ ■ ■

BRAD DEUTSER

WILEY

Published by John Wiley & Sons, Inc., Hoboken, New Jersey
Published simultaneously in Canada

For general information about our other products and services, please contact our Customer Care Department within the United States at (800) 762-2974, outside the United States at (317) 572-3993 or fax (317) 572-4002.

Wiley publishes in a variety of print and electronic formats and by print-on-demand. Some material included with standard print versions of this book may not be included in e-books or in print-on-demand. If this book refers to media such as a CD or DVD that is not included in the version you purchased, you may download this material at http://booksupport.wiley.com. For more information about Wiley products, visit www.wiley.com.

Library of Congress Cataloging-in-Publication Data

Names: Deutser, Brad, 1965– author.
Title: Leading clarity : the breakthrough strategy to unleash people, profit and performance / by Brad Deutser.
Description: Hoboken, New Jersey : John Wiley & Sons, Inc., [2018] | Includes index. |
Identifiers: LCCN 2017057355 (print) | LCCN 2017058928 (ebook) | ISBN 9781119457268 (pdf) | ISBN 9781119457244 (epub) | ISBN 9781119457251 (cloth)
Subjects: LCSH: Organizational effectiveness. | Strategic planning. | Leadership.
Classification: LCC HD58.9 (ebook) | LCC HD58.9 .D478 2018 (print) | DDC 658.4/012–dc23
LC record available at https://lccn.loc.gov/2017057355

Cover Design: Wiley

Printed in the United States of America

10 9 8 7 6 5 4 3 2 1

This book is dedicated to all who believe in the magic of clarity.

Contents

INTRODUCTION:
THE CLARITY CONUNDRUM

E very day, as leaders, we are faced with critical decisions as we navigate the constantly changing world around us. We understand, and reluctantly accept, that the manner in which we address the swirling winds around us will ultimately determine the success of our people, our company, and ourselves.

To many of us, the words *chaos*, *uncertainty*, and *change* immediately bring a twinge of anxiety and fear. We often hear of going *through* change, but we are never going to outrun or outlast change. Chaos is often served for breakfast as we hear the morning news, battle the commute, or have a carefully planned day hijacked by an urgent matter of utmost importance. Chaos is always going to find us and surround us, threatening at times to impale or drown us. Uncertainty takes a different tactic with the drip-drip-drip of things we can't control and the overwhelming-ness of perceived powerlessness. We desperately summon our best resources and release an arsenal of force, only to find that each effort brings more, and often greater, uncertainty.

The dynamics of change, chaos, and uncertainty are an integral part of the vitality that is business, and even more so, life. While the sheer force of change, uncertainty, and chaos swirls around us, we grasp for insight through both traditional and new measures of success. But with all the business tools and approaches that are routinely deployed, there is one outlier that is consistently misunderstood, misapplied, and vastly underrated. While it may be harder to measure than those most often relied on to create stability, it has been shown to improve performance, profitability, and ultimately, the viability of a company. What is this mystery function that serves from the root through every stage of growth and expansion and is arguably one of the most overlooked indicators of success available to individuals and companies today?

CLARITY

Clarity operates on the truth that everything is connected. We are never going to "have" clarity. It isn't ours to own. Clarity isn't an arrival point, a vista, or a destination. Leaders often work feverishly in attempts to communicate their way to clarity or to quickly design stratagems that may bring clarity while the illusion of control distracts us. These faulty ideas sometimes prompt us to impose or find our way *to* clarity by measuring profitability, shoring up our funding, calling for innovation, or preaching the need for greater timing. These tactics are accompanied by an endless list of acronyms applied to seemingly critical factors. But that is all data, not clarity. Why the impulse to seek clarity and how do we miss it in a fog of details and misdirected actions or grasp for it too late, just as it drifts beyond our reach? It is often because we never understood the value that clarity delivers or did the work that clarity requires. Many of us can recite a dramatic moment when clarity landed on us, out of the blue. I'm sure you've heard, or perhaps even used expressions like, "I had this moment of clarity," or "It suddenly hit me like a lightning bolt." We often mistake inspiration or identify a critical component that is a piece of a larger whole as clarity itself. We proclaim titles or attach labels and organize components into buckets, thinking that will coax clarity into our scope. I know that clarity is not a destination or something that arrives in a moment with a big "aha," or even a well-organized, perfectly labeled collection of pieces and parts. Clarity is a conundrum, a puzzle that needs to be solved, a bit of a brain tease that sings out to us in a siren's call but somehow escapes our attention.

I'm Brad Deutser, and nearly 20 years ago, I began to understand that many of the business problems I was encountering with companies large and small, privately owned and publicly traded, nonprofit and for profit, were all emerging from a common source—a lack of clarity. It isn't about spreadsheets, profits, or even sustainability. Clarity is the foundational fabric that weaves together dreams, goals, initiatives, concerns, challenges, and triumphs. Clarity is all about *people*. People make organizations. It is how we hang tough when called upon to do so, tear when we can't align, and bring forward something wonderful when the weave works. Clarity can't be simply communicated. It needs structure and has to be constructed.

I've built a vibrant business based on one dynamic that encompasses many: At Deutser, we teach others to lead with *clarity*. Our company thrives in times of uncertainty, ambiguity, change, and chaos. Our sweet spot is found in the "gray areas" of transition, which can manifest itself in many different ways inside an organization. You may recognize these transition opportunities as a new leader taking the helm, a new strategic plan being instituted across the company or any of a host of growth or change initiatives. Each is expected to bring a more vibrant future, but each also is wrought with a measure of unease and ambiguity.

While other consulting firms look for what is broken in times like these, we use positivity, more specifically, the fundamentals of positive psychology, to amplify and activate what works inside an organization to drive performance. Our work is designed to uncover the DNA and soul of an organization, its leaders, and the people who make it thrive, and we inspire and guide them to recognize whatever is most needed. It's the clarity we achieve through our process that allows us to help define, shape, improve, and protect a company, allowing them to create, stabilize, and enhance their organization … from the inside out.

Our clients represent a multitude of industries, including healthcare, media, energy and industrial services, retail, education, professional services, private equity, and not-for-profit organizations with an immense span of societal contributions. While the components for each are wildly different, we have created an ability to lead others to operate in clarity that is measurable, repeatable, and reliable. It is this methodology, developed over decades of work and research with hundreds of top businesses and tens of thousands of individuals, that I share with you in this book. Now, for the first time, we are sharing the tools and processes that previously have been available only to Deutser clients and client communities, developed through our research and experience using a unique, multidisciplinary approach.

At Deutser, we take a holistic approach to gain insight into clarity. I saw early in this endeavor that experts from various disciplines bring unique points of view, and by working collaboratively, we could interlace a foundational fabric for creating distinctive pathways fed by energy fields to desired outcomes. In some cases, we are involved in discovering and defining what makes up those dreams and desires. Deutser client teams include an organizational anthropologist, business consultant, organizational psychologist, digital and media strategist, and graphic designer. Each of their unique backgrounds contributes to strategically framing questions and evaluating the answers, providing more depth and insight to the data examined. The outcomes we deliver are derived from data that represents the answers to these questions from employees at every level—not just the executives who are emotionally connected to the brand or the organization and as such, less likely to objectively analyze what is going on within the hearts and minds of the people who make up the organization.

Instead of *finding* clarity, we know and understand that real value occurs when you, and ultimately your organization, are *in* clarity, which is a state that has both a form and methodology that can be relied on and can facilitate quick, and sometimes effortless, recalibration when faced with challenge. Being *in* clarity opens a way of creating personal capital that allows you to be steady in any storm. Considered as a destination, clarity can be lost or obscured the moment the landscape changes, or the environmental factors dim your view. In clarity, we can see all factors, recognize them for what they are and what they can become, and create connections that can be relied on to establish or reestablish equilibrium and an environment for growth.

THE PEOPLE FACTOR

Many leaders rely heavily on strategy and mistake it as that one overarching factor that reaches every aspect of the organization. Logic dictates that strategy is a highly prized component leading to business success. CEOs assemble their teams and build strategic plans that, on paper, make complete sense. But those same plans rarely take into account the reality of the people who are expected to execute them and the inability to add yet additional responsibilities to an already overly taxed workforce. This reinforces the belief that organizations aren't dysfunctional; people are. In fact, we have long believed that all organizations exist to serve someone's self-interest. If leaders are not in touch with what's happening with their people, and their people aren't aligned with the organization's expectations, then the cultural fabric is weak and it's only a matter of time until the business will suffer. Ninety percent of startups fail—most often having little to do with strategy. What does this have to do with clarity? Everything.

When organizations encounter significant change or experience chaos, companies need to protect their people. We have worked with hundreds of organizations around the world, confirming our theory that when a company is *in* clarity, the clear articulation and execution of culture becomes one of the foundational elements to driving organizational performance. The best time to articulate, cultivate, protect, and shape your culture is before you're faced with critical decisions related to growth, transition, or crisis. If you wait to address your culture until you're confronted with an economic downturn, a threat from a competitor, or an unexpected reputational issue, the instability within the organization will amplify any wave of challenge and can destabilize and threaten the organization itself.

As organizations face unprecedented uncertainty in the current business, political, and social climate, the speed of change increases the pressure to perform. This forces leaders to make decisions based on short-term goals and gains that oftentimes sacrifice long-term growth. As a result, employee engagement decreases when they see a disconnect between the corporate vision and operational realities. This breeds negativity and a workforce that is out of alignment, opening the door to dysfunction and a toxic environment of disengaged employees, subcultures, alliances, people with their own motives, potential lawsuits, low productivity, and high turnover. This devolution can leave leadership unable to attract and retain the best talent and struggle to overcome a misaligned workforce, which can make it virtually impossible for the organization to reach its full potential.

Companies in many industries are facing this crisis right now. Boards are demanding quarterly profits, which pressures leaders to make decisions that could potentially jeopardize the long-term value of the organization. When incentives for leaders are different from incentives for the employees, the organization can be weakened to the point of putting the quality of products and services at risk.

What starts happening when clarity is *actively* pursued? It gives leaders a tool with which to more effectively lead. It gives everybody a place to unite, creating employees who are better-performing and more engaged, happier, and increasingly committed rather than merely compliant. It gives the external constituents of a business, including customers, vendors, and partners, something more defined, authentic, and aligned with which to connect. Clarity delivers an organization that is fully functioning on all cylinders. Clarity delivers results.

Clarity itself has an elegance, an understanding that creates a series of connections that capture hopes, dreams, goals, intentions, foresight, insight, planning, possibilities, and the realization that many parts must come together in a spectacular way. It is the power grid that generates having the right energy in the right percentage for what is needed to excel. Clarity becomes central to your ability to not only visualize, but actualize your performance. Without a deep belief that your dreams are possible, in fact, highly probable, you will continually become tangled by fuzzy thinking and what I call circuit breakers.

Circuit Breakers

In clarity, we can see the brilliance of energy flowing throughout leaders and individuals, and we experience a deep understanding that everything is connected. This natural flow of energy that leaders are able to maintain is fundamental to their ability to lead clarity. We tend, however, to easily activate our long-developed coping skills, habits, and style under stress. We typically think that our well-worn, previously depended-on antics aid our process. They can create, instead, circuit breakers that interrupt the flow of energy and break our connection with our employees, our company, and ourselves.

These "breaks" can result in misguided or conflicting directions. In clarity, we produce the optimal environment with energy calibrated at the right frequency directed to the right places, which facilitates a constant and vibrant flow. This flow is what drives the performance of the leader and subsequently the organization.

While some circuit breakers may be individualized, the 12 universal circuit breakers that we've identified in our work include:

Fear

This great "gotcha" that grabs our gut and shows up at the worst times is nondiscriminatory in that its presence can be felt in winning or losing. Even success brings fear about what will change and move us out of our well-rutted comfort. Fear shows up when we finally get that promotion we've been working so hard for as we worry (a byproduct of fear) how it will change life. We worry about whether we can actually do the job, or if now, under increased scrutiny, we will be more vulnerable. The list goes on and on. Whatever the instigating factor or the root cause of fear, the result is the same. It has an underbelly that churns. Some part of your energy and spirit is choppy and it creates starts and stops and inconsistencies that send mixed messages and efforts that are half efforts or at best, good enough. You fear that flying too high can bring you down and with a loud crash, but all fear is creating breakages or missed connections.

Ambivalence

This mix of feelings creates misguided direction or no direction as the pull toward multiple options or contradictory ideas fries the energy pathways. Ambivalence leaves us in a perpetual search for something and we can feel the sting of disenfranchisement and being left outside of our connection. In our frazzled energy, we agitate smooth operations by offering conflicting messages and a lack of decision making or solid recommendations. We always leave room to cover mistakes and manage risk, leaving the door ajar to abandon ship and try something else rather than going all in on one initiative.

Clutter

It doesn't matter whether the bog is mental, organizational, physical, or anything else that can become disordered; clutter impedes a direct path. Sure, you might be able to make it through the maze of clutter, but there are opportunities missed while on detour and often, efficiency lost. Sometimes, you can't find the path or create one as energy and resources are expended that could be appropriated elsewhere instead of being used merely "figuring it out." That same energy can be redirected to bigger ideas with far better design with more promise of bringing extraordinary outcomes rather than just the temporary "yay" of finding your way. And to where, exactly?

Labeling

We often employ labeling when we don't know what else to do. Labeling gives us a momentary false sense of control, thinking that if we can name it or categorize it, we can influence or perhaps even control it. This energy can lead to a fracture, causing us to completely miss something unique about what we're not understanding. Labeling soothes by giving form to something and reassures us that we then know what to do with it or about it. Labeling makes it more real to us. Where labeling becomes a circuit breaker is where it recreates what is already familiar to us because in its very genesis, we labeled it as something already known. Tolerating ambiguity has been shown to be a part of highly functioning mental health. Being in clarity allows space where we wait for what we don't quite understand to emerge, which keeps energy available and flowing rather than being boxed in, covered up, or mistakenly shelved through what's already known. Labeling serves to define and often constrict something that hasn't yet taken shape. It can interrupt the evolution of an idea, project, endeavor, or a glorious and unexpected awakening.

Doubt

A loss of faith or lack of belief shuts down our access to source. Believers are willing to trust and invest in something that is bigger and different. To do big things and make positive changes, doubt must be bypassed. Legacies aren't built on doubt. Sometimes the act of "doing" alone can shift energy and keep doubt at arm's length. Trust can assuage doubt. Most often, as is our core belief, people prefer to work with people, teams, and organizations that they know, like, and trust. Certainly, there is room for constant additions to the roster, but to enter those relationships or any partnership with doubt creates maladjustments and cuts off sustenance in the work. Doubt starves the life flow of creativity and expansion. Trust and belief can lift you through tough times and circumstances when you are tested. Doubt operates as a heavy, dense energy that keeps you tethered to old ways and old thinking as you drag your entire cache of outdated business along with you.

Impatience

We like to see things happening. Activity feeds our energy and we like the positive reinforcement of progress. Our sales sheets look great when they are full of calls and orders. Our occupancy rate reinforces that we're doing a good job. And, our well-documented everything convinces us that all is being carried out as dictated. All activity. But what about action? Action is the energy that moves us forward, not just keeping us participating. When we flap our wings of activity without producing any action, we grow impatient. In clarity, we develop the practice of strategic patience in an environment in which business practices often favor short-term gains over long-term sustainability. Strategic patience occurs when you are thoughtful, purposeful, intentional, and favor actions that make an impact. Strategic patience also teaches you to trust while strategically harvesting resources ready for a better time, opportunity, or the right team member who can generate a greater outcome. Strategic patience ensures that you have the reserves to stay on course toward your desired outcome, no matter how treacherous. Impatience may just take you right into the swamp where you can be eaten alive, or at least be in need of a costly rescue. Impatience creates a frenetic energy that results in unnecessary or ill-advised risk. The need for constant activity, often accompanied by micromanagement, depletes resources and increases irritation.

Boredom

While many hyperbolic energies are recognized to create disruption and distraction in business, boredom, in its lack of inspiration or higher thought, is perhaps one of the deadliest circuit breakers. To start with, it is insidious. It lazily reaches for the low-hanging fruit. It performs at a level at which it is just good enough not to be noticed or called out and therefore can continue to underperform. In any industry in which safety is important, it can result in accidents, injuries, or death—death of a business, a bottom line, or a life. Boredom shows itself through a lack of power and as a weak signal through an organization. It is the six feet of bridge missing that you automatically count on to be there, that can plunge you into deep waters. It is that tiny screw that is loose that rattles the structure until it destabilizes. Boredom is a circuit breaker because it doesn't produce enough energy to make a connection. It is characterized by the "lack of." The damage can be seen throughout an organization, but comes clearly into view as critical connections are established and circuit breaks are exposed.

Conflict

Power struggles are characterized by a clash of energy directed at people rather than goals or dreams. Conflicting values can certainly be the spark that ignites a power struggle, but they are more often about claiming resources and perceived territory than they are about truly hashing out the differences in values. Conflict can also be a positive because it adds a burst of energy, but that energy can overwhelm and set off a chain reaction of unsuitable and undesirable toxic particles that can shower your group with something that leaves them needing a good cleanse. Conflict can also grow out of greed or a departure that takes you too far from your root and breaks your connection to what nourishes.

Overconfidence

Leaders thrive on confidence. We absolutely need to be able to make decisions, believe in ourselves and others, and discern

.the best options for our companies. Where this attribute becomes a circuit breaker is when confidence becomes arrogance, self-absorption, peacocking, and a baseless feeling of invincibility. On the practical side, it can blind you and close you off to important information or prompt you to make impulsive decisions without securing critical details and input. On the people side, it can make you obnoxious, difficult, unapproachable, and someone with whom no one wants to work. It can close you off to empathy for others because you project your abilities onto someone else and miss that they are struggling, or even worse, you judge them instead of connecting with them.

Physical Depletion

Leaders, like the great marathon runners, must deal with the real consequences of the daily mental and physical assaults that they are so uniquely expected to address. Leaders are constantly tapped to bridge worlds and problems. They are in the same moment surviving and setting up future success. While they believe that survival is the only option, they ignore the personal toll it takes on them. It is like the proverbial creative high—that high continues to build to a climax before the inevitable crash. It is simply not sustainable, which leaders will all admit, but few proactively address. The conscious decision of when to expend energy in the workplace and when to reserve it is an art, and sadly, to some, mistaken as a sign of weakness. We are trained to lead and serve on the frontlines, never showing weakness. Yet, the increasing occurrences of unhealthy workplaces, mental health issues, and illnesses, including obesity, are all directly or indirectly related to the action and expectation of the leader. Physical depletion is a factor that defines energy and requires a thoughtful plan for recovery.

Inference

We live in a world in which inference is ever-present. Conversations are short. Attention spans are even shorter. We are talked to or talked around, rather than engaging in meaningful dialog. Today's world prizes headlines and bite-sized phrases rather than the full narrative that more aptly provides color and definition. I encounter situations every day in which I am forced to catch myself as I begin to attach my own meaning to someone else's thoughts or words or lack of words. I fill in the blanks left by others, often, when there are no blanks to fill. Social media only takes this to a different, even more, ambiguous level. In the social media world, brevity is revered, punctuation is nonexistent, and voice left to the reader to discern—leaving the most basic words to be characterized and mischaracterized—is it Fine? Fine, or Fine!? More and more, we find ourselves ascribing our own voice, our own reasoning, and our own meaning—moving understanding further away from its intended destination.

Resources

There are constraints that we each are challenged to navigate on a daily basis. No matter how much or little of something you have in life or in business, we are each constantly evaluating and measuring—against ourselves, our friends, our peers, and our competitors. It is a daily exercise to try to balance the various riches, deficits, and constraints with which we are faced. The balancing act in itself is not a circuit breaker—rather, it becomes one when the exercise consumes our thinking, redirects our thoughts, and stops our flow of positive energy. Time can become a circuit breaker as we edit our possibilities because we simply "do not have the time to try that." Time is one of the many resources we must constantly be aware of as we evaluate our healthy energy pathways. Others include financial resources, real or perceived, as we prioritize our future through a financial lens. There are times when we don't pursue the development of an idea because we can't afford it or don't have the people to implement it. Is it that we do not have the resources or are we unwilling to fundamentally rethink the conventionality of our execution plan? We have found there are many ways to get to the desired outcome and how we interact with and overcome this circuit breaker goes a long way to dictating our success.

These are the most prevalent circuit breakers that we see leaders and their workforce work to navigate daily. Disconnected thinking, the status quo, and stress serve as other circuit breakers.

Leaders who strive to be in clarity understand the forces that break the necessary and natural flow of energy for them and their organizations. They recognize its impact on them and the people they lead. And, they understand its direct connection to culture, which plays a defining role in driving performance and is the first entry point to being in clarity. We introduce circuit breakers here because this purposeful flow of energy is not only fundamental for a leader leading clarity, but something that each leader controls on a daily and even minute-by-minute basis. Without this energy, it is challenging to successfully navigate, much less lead, clarity.

YOUR CLARITY CONUNDRUM

As you consider entering a space where clarity can be created, sustained, and grown, let's look at some specific points at which our clients sought and achieved clarity. This may serve as a catalyst for how you might begin your own experience through the power grid of clarity that we'll create in the coming chapters. Or, you can continue as an observer as the material begins to resonate and you join in our own creation of clarity. I've arranged these by topics but the examples could go on for many pages. Perhaps you might see something that parallels your current Clarity Conundrum.

A Need for New Vision

There is nothing more defining than the creation of a new long-range vision for a company. It is a critical component of being in organizational clarity. We often see organizations simply focus on day-to-day operations, rarely looking forward and fatefully overlooking their lack of vision. Since clarity brings connection, a lack of vision results in misguided or nonexistent directions, bringing unintentional shifts. Outside of clarity, many will see these neutral points as contributing to chaos, uncertainty, and change. But in clarity, we see them as powerful signals that it is time for sending some energy toward vision.

A healthcare organization needs to raise $50M through philanthropy, and in clarity, grows to understand that people don't give to operations, they give to big, aspirational, impactful ideas.

A technology company is reeling from its hostile takeover of its chief rival and wants to not only survive, but thrive.

A legacy retail company is stuck, showing 15 years of static sales in a highly competitive market. They want to become contenders but don't know where to start.

An identity crisis brews and bubbles over as one of the world's leading healthcare research and education centers has a dramatic drop in the critical U.S. News and World Report *rankings, and they need to regain their standing.*

A fast-growing industrial services company needs to create a disruptive strategy to become an industry leader.

Leadership of a top not-for-profit health institution creates a long-range strategy that is inconsistent with research findings and organizational composition that can lead the group off purpose and off path.

One of the nation's leading colleges needs to transform its educational delivery model in answer to a dramatically changing educational landscape.

Repositioning

Organizations typically want to address repositioning with a redefined brand or corporate image, or when they want to introduce a new product, service, or new approach. They are working in these times to bring a new measure of clarity to their workforce and customer base.

A former first lady wants to reposition her cause and organization and become the driving force to address a critical societal issue affecting nearly 40 percent of the community.

One of the premier transportation companies in the world considers repositioning itself to keep their edge in the midst of significant industry change.

Merger

Clarity creates a new normal during and throughout the merger of companies, identities, and ideas. The lack of clarity often sends shockwaves instantly through all affected organizations, extending to the client or customer base. In these situations, the lack of clarity is often immediately known by the workforce, but acted out years later as poor performance and unrealized returns.

Two top health organizations merge systems without addressing critical cultural issues in both companies.

A new highly disruptive startup in the energy space acquires multiple companies simultaneously, placing culture above operations.

Acquisition

In today's business environment, corporate acquisitions have become not only the norm, but almost the expectation in many industries. Those acquired can often feel the sting of loss of history, culture, and continuity as they become part of something larger and with new dreams, goals, and ideas. The ability for these companies to achieve clarity across both organizations goes a long way to their ultimate collective ability to achieve the financial expectations established at the onset of the deal.

Previously family owned funeral homes are challenged with effective integration into a publicly traded company.

A national food franchiser positions its business for growth in order to be acquired.

A rapidly growing services company with new private equity backing is forced to retard sales to ease alignment with other investments outside the industry.

Failing/Stuck at a Plateau

Failing or being stuck has to be one of the most uncomfortable times in business. It can be paralyzing, which only exacerbates the situation. Clarity can drive you through tough challenges and on to amazing results and outcomes, leaving the past far, far behind.

A company with feuding leaders fails to move the company forward over a decade, losing market share as competitors move in and take market share and the leadership position.

An educational institution experiences declining enrollment.

A health institution's leadership was given a hard stop by the Board of Trustees, granting a mere 90 days to turn its operations around or consider closing the system and releasing the more than four thousand employees.

A large urban school district faces the challenge of starting the school year at an 1800-teacher deficit.

Safety

There are few areas in which a lack of clarity has more devastating and often irrevocable results.

An international energy production company needs to introduce a new safety initiative that will change the culture of an operation-focused organization.

A company faced with a potential terrorist threat needs to protect their people, assets, and ongoing operation.

Critical for Survival

Coming into clarity can bring you out of denial to recognize that the only direction is forward. This forward pathway is often what is required for organizational sustainability and growth.

A respected museum is caught between the ideals of its successful past and the emerging needs of an unknown future.

A leading healthcare institution needs a succession plan for continued growth and long-term viability.

Crisis

Crises arrive as unexpected, unwanted, and often undeserved events. Clarity serves as the rudder through crisis and can transform an accidental or situational upending to a defined and deliberate elevation of circumstance.

A series of high-profile industry accidents calls into question the viability of the industry.

A murder takes place on a university campus.

A leader is accused of the misappropriation of funds.

An elected board member is revealed as one who has worked to undermine the institution he was entrusted to serve and protect.

Leadership

Leaders need clarity. Without it, the organization will be misguided and, despite best efforts, will eventually fail.

A new president discovers data that shows one of the highest performer's behaviors is wholly inconsistent with the organization's values.

A new CEO, recognizing a key product was 8 percent of the business compared to industry standards of 24 percent, wills the organization to increase sales.

A founder of a company recognizes the value proposition of working against his leadership team.

We each have our own clarity conundrums on a daily, weekly, and monthly basis. How we, as leaders, understand, embrace, and address our conundrums goes a long way to determining our success and the success of the people we are entrusted to lead. As we will explore in this book, there are many variables, mostly out of our control, that will not only not change, but continue to grow exponentially. It is how we tackle the ambiguity and challenge that they present that will define performance. The sheer pace and ever-evolving societal, technological, and political nuances, pressures, and landmines that leaders must constantly navigate are real—and they make our decisions more complex, and often, more heavily weighted with high stakes. Every decision, every action, every word is wrought with consequence. Ambiguity is real and can best be addressed by its most potent antidote, *CLARITY*.

Clarity requires our focused attention and effort to become accessible. On a daily basis, it is easier to slip into a clarity conundrum, as our minds and hearts shift rapidly and we attempt to multitask to comprehend what is occurring. Multitasking and trying to juggle everything at once leaves us in a dazed and disintegrated state of being, incapable of seeing the bigger picture. Therefore, it is paramount to understand each individual component in its own right, because clarity is a holistic process, where overall alignment is only possible after careful consideration of the parts involved.

Therefore, as you move forward with this book, I encourage you to be mindful of the magnitude of clarity and the dynamic interactions taking place behind the scenes. Clarity itself grows like a mustard seed, which at its origin represents the tiniest seed but has the potential to grow exponentially. I hope that you will be open to explore each of the concepts we introduce as they unfold. To some, the lack of a linear approach to clarity can raise questions. However, when you are able to take in the totality of all things that impact clarity, you will see the holistic power it creates. After all, it took me and my team of consultants years of thorough research and interaction with clients for this concept to manifest itself.

That being said, the realization of clarity has transformed the way we conduct our business; it has enhanced the performance and stature of companies time and time again. The pathway to clarity is different for every company, due to the unique identity and foundation that make up each entity. It begins with building your "box"—defining the facets of your business that distinguish you from the rest. This becomes the vehicle that is driven by your collective team into the future, which propels your productivity to the next level. You will also formulate your distinct identity (the foundation that supports everything you do) and create the dimensions of your "window." Through this window, your company will be able to perceive the external factors that affect your company's performance, so you can adapt and prepare for what's down the road accordingly.

Through this formulation process, your company will gain an understanding of every component which is paramount to your success. With that in mind, we will also create the organizational levers that are used to drive positive change and motivate a broader impact for your company. Altogether, this inside-out approach yields the potential for alignment, where all the components and parts are working seamlessly together and firing on all cylinders. The benefits of alignment are endless; it provides an integration and interconnectedness between your people and your company mission and combines all the dynamic forces together into one flowing source of energy.

We encourage and propose to you that if you will follow us in creating your own space in which you, too, can be in clarity, we will lead you to explore and experience results that our many clients have enjoyed, such as:

- Improved bottom-line performance
- Facilitation for growth—personal and professional
- Ensured alignment within your organization
- Increased customer satisfaction
- Allowing leaders to unite merged institutions
- Improved safety and wellbeing of the workforce

- Increased employee retention

- Advanced employee recruitment

- Enhanced individual employee performance

- Palpable happiness throughout the organization

By tying everything in your company together and unifying its collective efforts, you will ultimately elevate the level of outcomes that you can and will capture. By setting yourself up to exist in a state of clarity more frequently, you effectively establish a new precedent for success and expand the horizons that your company can explore. In essence, being in clarity positions you in a place where magic is bound to happen—in the results you seek and for the company you keep.

CHAPTER 1

Think Inside the Box

The concept of "thinking outside the box" has been the go-to, we're-all-about-it superstar for decades. TED Talks offer up a chorus of praise for this invocation to innovation, certain to bring greater success to businesses and organizations. Proponents say thinking outside the box fires up creativity and that it can result in inventive solutions to an organization's most nagging problems. But for all the positive promotion it's received over the years, that philosophy may be putting too much emphasis on the wrong side of the box.

I believe, and our work has found, that you have a much better chance of success if you understand the parameters you're working *within* as an organization, and then see if you can stretch the box to meet your goals and vision. In other words, taking into account real-world limitations—such as budget constraints, industry regulations, looming deadlines—can actually help to spark creativity by keeping it focused rather than using an open-ended, anything-goes approach that doesn't reliably result in ideas that can be implemented from a practical standpoint.

Thinking outside the box sounds like a great way to spur creativity and innovation, but it can take you in directions far removed from your true goals or what you can actually accomplish. We find it to have ambiguity in that there are no boundaries, there are too many variables, and too many unknowns. When working in the box, your playing field is more defined and there is greater understanding of specifics and their possible impact on your desired outcome. There is also more empathy and connectivity in the box because there is definition. The box perspective is not only critical for the leader to define the parameters of the organization, it is equally important for the employees to have clarity around the business focus and the elements that directly affect them. Furthermore, the box provides a critical context for the board and leader to work together and create commonality around the expectations of the company. The box provides a form of clarity for all to grab hold of and work toward. The powerful point is that the box is of your own making. There are no rules or regulations with the box. There is no size requirement. Only you can determine the right box for your company, one that is big enough for your wildest performance objectives, but focused enough to allow you to achieve the goals you establish. You should also understand that while the sides of the box exist, they can be permeable, to let things flow in and out, and be flexible, to expand or contract when deemed necessary; but, once inside, each element serves to interact with the whole. This in itself contributes to being in clarity. While society celebrates wild, outside-the-box ideas, even though most of us don't have the creativity or vision to really be far outside, the complexity of today's business environment dictates that you must be more focused, more purposeful, more connected, and more strategic. The definition of your box and willingness to push the parameters inside the box is therefore critical to your long-term sustainable performance.

BUILD YOUR BOX

The construct of each box is unique. We have helped companies across the world devise strategies to create an original and appropriate box for their industry, markets, products, services, and realities. While the challenges for each company are unique, the components and framework are consistent. Let's examine what each of the four sides of the box represents and how they can be defined to ensure alignment with the organization. The four sides of the box are:

1. Direction

2. Operations

3. People

4. Engagement

These four components are the critical factors that contribute to and directly affect performance and culture. Organizations that put the effort into defining their box by actively planning for, talking about, and populating each of these sides are those that can uncover clarity—the gem inside the box—and through the processes presented in this book, drive vibrant and lasting performance.

Now that we have four sides of the box, it is important to provide greater definition by populating each side with three dimensions, each critical to organizational performance. When you think inside the box, you'll have a better handle on the organization's structure, strategy, and culture as well as their undeniable impact and influence on each other. (See Figure 1.1) That in turn will help determine the best way to shape, grow, and stretch the organization's box to meet and ultimately exceed goals. While thinking outside the box offers the allure of freedom without constraint, thinking inside the box actually gives you structure and an approach to thoughtful expansion, which provides more effective thinking freedom with the foundational mediums from which to springboard. Working inside the box generates collective impact where you can identify and envision your future state as well as understand your current state. We believe that it is the expectations leaders set that serve to close the gap between their current state and desired future state.

As we create the box and provide more robust understanding of the composition of each side, we have identified 12 dimensions

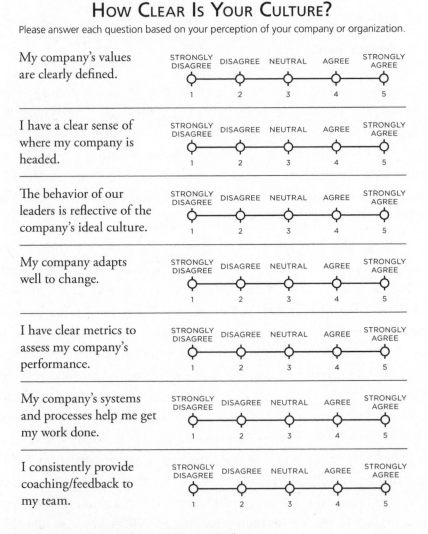

Figure 1.1   How Clear Is Your Culture

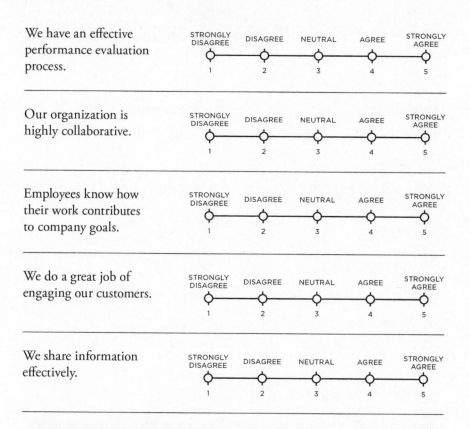

We have an effective performance evaluation process.

STRONGLY DISAGREE	DISAGREE	NEUTRAL	AGREE	STRONGLY AGREE
1	2	3	4	5

Our organization is highly collaborative.

STRONGLY DISAGREE	DISAGREE	NEUTRAL	AGREE	STRONGLY AGREE
1	2	3	4	5

Employees know how their work contributes to company goals.

STRONGLY DISAGREE	DISAGREE	NEUTRAL	AGREE	STRONGLY AGREE
1	2	3	4	5

We do a great job of engaging our customers.

STRONGLY DISAGREE	DISAGREE	NEUTRAL	AGREE	STRONGLY AGREE
1	2	3	4	5

We share information effectively.

STRONGLY DISAGREE	DISAGREE	NEUTRAL	AGREE	STRONGLY AGREE
1	2	3	4	5

ADD UP YOUR SCORES TO FIND YOUR OVERALL CLARITY SCORE
SCORING LOGIC

54-60

ACTUALIZED CULTURE
Fully embraced and lived out by all individuals.

48-53

PURPOSEFUL CULTURE
Well-defined, on its way to being embraced.

42-47

ACCIDENTAL CULTURE
Lacks definition and is an unintended byproduct of every employee.

41 OR LESS

POTENTIALLY MALADAPTIVE CULTURE
Misdirected and toxic, benefiting the few at the expense of the many.

(three for each side) that bring color and definition to each of the four sides of the box. We have listed here the side of the box with the corresponding dimensions:

Direction:

1. Vision and values

2. Strategy

3. Leadership

Operations:

4. Adaptability

5. Performance management

6. Systems and processes

People:

7. Employee clarity and fit

8. Customer focus

9. Communication effectiveness

Engagement:

10. Coaching and development

11. Talent management

12. Team capabilities

Side One: Direction

Without strong leadership, established and exhibited values, clear vision, and a strategy to achieve the vision, an organization will not be successful. The findings from our research consistently demonstrate that without direction employees become disengaged and less productive, negatively affecting culture and performance—theirs and the company's. Direction affects every aspect of the company and its ability to connect with and move its people to a shared vision of where the company is going. As you will read throughout this book, it is not simply the environment that defines outcomes; rather it is the expectations that leaders set that play a fundamental role in driving individual and collective performance.

Dimension: Vision and Values

All too often, we, as leaders, think that this dimension will take care of itself. A clearly defined and stated vision is the first step to aligning the organization. Vision is one of the most important skills of leadership and flows from the leader down. A strong and well-defined vision creates a momentum that compels others to follow and actively promote it through their work. If there is no top-down vision, departments, teams, and individuals are going it alone to attempt to create something of value. Vision unites, inspires, and sets the tone for higher thinking throughout the organization. But, the great caveat with vision—if it is not defined with clear expectations, it is only a grouping of often carefully crafted words. We must say what we mean, then define it and be clear about what success will look like.

Values set the standards of what is important to your company. Yes, it seems like there are values that all companies share, such as integrity, creating profit, building exemplary products, or contributing to a community through service. Having clearly articulated values that distinguish your company from others in the industry, however, is crucial for employees and customers to directly identify with. These cannot be values that live on cards that employees carry or on posters affixed on walls throughout the organization, but real values that connect the employee with the heart and soul of the company.

Think about your company's vision and values with the following statements. How does your organization perform?

- Employees have a shared vision of the company's future.

- Employees know what the company's core values are.

- The company's values are typically reflected in employees' behaviors.

Dimension: Strategy

This dimension is familiar to all leaders, but each may define it differently. To us, your strategy tells the plan of where your company is headed—it is your definition of change. It gives form to a general idea or plan, and informs it through assigning specific language to what it is you plan to achieve and specific pathways describing how you are going to go about it. These seem like tried-and-true business tools, and they are, but we often find that there is either no clearly communicated strategy in place or one that is too complex to implement; and if there is a clear plan, it isn't clear who is responsible for what, and how it collectively fits together. In short, too many strategic plans are developed, intricately built out, and sit on shelves in the C-suite. Leadership needs a strategy that they can collectively believe in, rely on, and act on. Strategy sets the direction with specific actions to take you toward your vision.

Think about your company's strategy with the following three statements. How does your organization perform?

- I have confidence in the strategic direction of the company.

- Leadership clearly communicates the strategic plan to employees.

- Our strategy is updated regularly to keep the company competitive.

Dimension: Leadership

Leadership is foundational to clarity. It is the highest and most reliable indicator of success. Purposeful culture is led. The ideas, values, and strategies in this quadrant begin to define a purposeful culture that is inextricably linked to overall organizational reliability and performance. Culture happens, with or without your attention. It is up to the leadership to establish a purposeful culture and empower a consistently productive working environment.

Think about your company's leadership with the following statements. How do your organization's leaders perform?

- Leadership inspires and motivates me to work hard to accomplish company goals.

- Overall, I have confidence in the decisions made by our leadership.

- Leadership encourages new ideas and problem solving.

I had the opportunity to interact with the CEO and board chair of a highly successful international retailer experiencing dramatic challenges to the company. Their once-proud legacy was under attack by a new CEO empowered to change the very fabric that defined the company. Yet, with each change the leader made, the organization moved further and further away from its long-standing traditions. The loyal employees became disconnected from the organization. And, more, the customers felt left behind as evidenced by decreasing sales. What was central to the issue was the very clear definition of the box in which they had always operated and the fact that the new CEO was brought in to be completely outside the box and reinvent the brand. But the leader's focus was new for the sake of being new as opposed to rethinking key organizational elements like the brand, delivery model, and culture. The new leader understood the pressures coming, brought on by the rapid change in market share gains of the mega-retailers and could see that brick-and-mortar retail would be increasingly squeezed by this shift in consumer behavior. While the leader was clearer than anyone in her company that the old service delivery method, focused heavily on direct mail catalogs, was in jeopardy, she chose to overhaul everything at once, including the well-established, clearly defined brand. This avalanche of change for a legacy brand resulted in the alienation of prideful employees and loyal customers who wanted the product the company had always delivered. The leader's out-of-the-box efforts brought the board into clarity about what it was they really wanted, which was very different from the idea of changing everything. The board and the new CEO eventually had to part ways. While the board wanted change, the change they got was too far outside the bounds of the company they loved and had jumped entirely out of the box of what they wanted. The company had the choice to, as we say, "change the people or change the people"—meaning change their behavior or change the actual individual's employment status with the company. Their solution was to change the people at the top and they immediately regained the trust of the workforce with a return to the long-standing culture and a fresh look inside their box.

Side Two: Operations

Here we measure the company's ability to respond to external changes, as well as employees' ability to respond to organizational changes. The performance management dimension gathers data regarding the organization's use of data to make management decisions. The final dimension asks questions to determine whether an organization's systems and processes are effective in helping employees do their work well.

Dimension: Adaptability

This dimension is directly related to change. As discussed in the Introduction, change is ongoing and something which we all are constantly navigating. Adaptability is a dimension about which you often experience the relevance of circuit breakers because they impede adaptability. In clarity, we recognize that we are always in a state of change, so adaptability and circuit breakers are fatefully linked. In a purposeful organization, the box creates an optimal environment in which adaptability is part of the way the company operates, not an individual struggle. Leadership identifies, anticipates, and makes way for adaptation as *part of* change instead of as a result of change.

Think about your company's ability to adapt with the following statements. How does your organization perform?

- The company responds well to change.
- Company changes usually have a positive impact on me.
- I am willing to question the norm to improve the way we do things.

The foundation of a national philanthropist had earned a reputation for generously doling resources out to every worthwhile cause in the region. Many organizations relied on their contributions. The foundation's leadership worked hard to establish and build a reputation of broad generosity and meeting many of the needs in the community. This was supported in both their words and actions. There was an undeniable pride by the leadership of the foundation from this reputation. For years, they were stuck in the ways of how they had always operated, with a fixed perspective on not only who they were, but in their minds, who they needed to remain. However, the philanthropist gained insight into the help they were providing and believed that the foundation could make a more meaningful impact by doing a lot for a little rather than their strategy of doing a little for a lot. The philanthropist tasked leadership with redefining the box in which they operated to now focus on four distinct areas where they could make a quantifiable difference. Rather than be all things to all people, the foundation became laser focused on the causes most near and dear to its purpose. While the organization defined its new box, the original leaders were unable to adapt to the redefined box. This led to new people at the top of the foundation, a new vision and strategy, new operational platforms, and new engagement techniques to identify the causes they will support within their box. They moved from being accidental, even though intentional to spread as much good as possible, to being purposeful in populating their box and focusing initiatives in clarity that met their vision and goals. The building of their box, and the adaptability that was required, has led to new energy in their mission and a clear definition as to the legacy they will leave.

Dimension: Performance Management

Operating in clarity means having clear data metrics in place that measure those behaviors, actions, and outcomes that are an integral part of key initiatives. Without the proper metrics, quality feedback and directional intelligence is impossible. Data metrics are imperative to leading an intentional operation. In clarity, we define what we need and perpetually revise as change occurs.

Think about your company's performance management capabilities with the following statements. How does your organization perform?

- We have performance measures to show us if the company is achieving our goals.

- The company uses performance data to make business decisions.

- The company constantly seeks ways to improve how we do our work.

Dimension: Systems and Processes

This dimension exists to streamline work. In most of the organizations with which we work, we initially find that the systems are outdated and the ever-quickening pace of short-term gains that has become the norm today destabilizes systems that are often found lagging behind what is needed to get ahead. As your directional quadrant is defined, you will need to determine if you have the right systems and process to streamline the path that your strategy will follow. What needs should you be anticipating that you're currently overlooking, which assist with adaptability? Can you tap your directional quadrant to strategize the creation of or update a system that is needed? Are you clear on what and when it will need to be ready and what it needs to support or produce? Systems and processes that do not serve to streamline become one of the circuit breakers as clutter.

Think about your company's systems and processes with the following statements. How does your organization perform?

- The company's systems and processes ensure high-quality work.

- The company's systems and processes distribute information in an effective way.

- The company regularly improves our processes so I can be effective.

Side Three: People

We believe that without the right people who are treated well and are well-supported, an organization cannot live up to its full potential. Ultimately, the people of a company are what motivate growth and sustain the parameters of the box that you define. Without their investment in the vision and their understanding of the pathways in place to reach optimal performance, your strategy will inevitably fall short of its expected outcomes.

Dimension: Coaching and Development

People want to feel valued. And, they want to positively contribute to the organization. The onus is on the leadership to recognize the talents, sometimes hidden in an employee, and help to elevate them to a new level of performance with focused coaching and development. Commitment to people becomes palpable when intentional.

Think about your company's coaching and development and fit with the following statements. How does your organization perform?

- My supervisor regularly meets with me to provide feedback and discuss my work.

- The company is committed to my professional learning and career development.

- The company provides clear pathways for advancement.

Dimension: Talent Management

This dimension is often one that brings a unique contradiction of both passion and dissatisfaction from employees in our initial interviews and data collection. We have seen how talent management is a critical factor in clarity as teams and individuals grapple with increasing demands placed on them, including the pace with which we work, technology updates and demands, and general uncertainty.

Think about your company's talent management with the following statements. How does your organization perform?

- My team is staffed appropriately to get our work done well.
- I consistently receive annual reviews of my performance.
- Promotions are granted on talent, not tenure.

Dimension: Team Capabilities

The term *capability* holds such promise. Aligned teams working in clarity find a boost in capability through organized effort. Clarity in teams makes the way for more open and honest communication. When collaboration and co-creation are valued, hired for, and expected, it releases the need to be the smartest person in the room. Teams add to clarity by providing sounding-boards for ideas and possibilities. Teams are especially important in high-potential events when reliance on one another exposes circuit breakers that need repair. Diversity in teams adds to clarity by working a problem from different angles and points of view. When you pair two people who normally wouldn't work on something together, you can gain insight and open a way to a third point of view that emerges from their work together. Clarity has a different agenda from just the individual elements involved.

Think about your employees' team capabilities with the following statements. How does your organization perform?

- The company has a spirit of teamwork and cooperation.
- Working in teams generates new ideas.
- Teamwork is a big part of how we get things done.

Side Four: Engagement

Our view of engagement focuses on having engaged employees but also examines the extent to which an organization engages with other stakeholders, both internal (including board members and volunteers, if applicable) or external (including clients or customers).

Dimension: Employee Clarity and Fit

Employees are frequently recruited and hired because of their knowledge, skills, and abilities. In clarity, we are looking for fit, which is a much better indicator of longevity and success. In addition to the requisite skillset, we hire, evaluate, and train based on shared values and core competencies. Employee engagement and satisfaction are enhanced when expectations and behaviors are clearly defined and communicated. Clarity ensures that every person has a place and a role that is compatible with their individual traits as well as the collective traits defining the company.

Think about your company's employees' clarity and fit with the following statements. How does your organization perform?

- My role, goals, and objectives are clearly defined.
- I have a good relationship with my co-workers.
- I take pride in my company's success.

Dimension: Customer Focus

Companies and customers enter into an exchange of expectations and delivery of goods and services. As with internal culture, these expectations can be clear and purposeful, or they develop unintentionally as either an informal or even a more formal social contract.

Think about your company's customer focus with the following statements. How does your organization perform?

- The company understands our clients' expectations.

- The company values feedback from our clients.

- Employees are empowered to solve client problems.

Dimension: Communication Effectiveness

We see the attempts of businesses trying to communicate their way to clarity every day. This is often the case when leaders haven't created the whole of their box and are looking for a quick fix. Effective, clear communication is a positive outcome of clarity, but it cannot be the primary driver. Clarity brings a whole other genre of communication that exceeds what is routinely experienced. In clarity, communication evokes a connection, a response, and establishes transparency and authenticity as its goal. With this style of communicating, everyone involved wants to interact with it and contribute to it. Communication effectiveness is predicated on a two-way dialog and genuine commitment to engagement.

Think about your company's communication effectiveness with the following statements. How does your organization perform?

- Lines of communication are open all the way to top management.

- Information passed down from leadership is detailed and accurate.

- I receive the right amount of information to do my job effectively.

For my own company, I recognized that whatever distinct industry our company was once a part, no longer existed. We started out as one thing and wandered for years, before defining our box and creating the clarity we help others achieve. We started as a strategic communications firm that dealt with highly complex issues. In fact, the more complex and multifaceted, the more they were in our wheelhouse. Our journey started with a basic understanding. We believed that in the 1980s, the advertising industry gave away the intellectual high ground to consultancies—basically saying, "You be smart and we'll be creative." We recognized this shift, but also understood we didn't fit in either world. It forced us to make a critical decision—did we want to be a local boutique focused on design and advertising, or did we want to be a bigger player in the space of consultancy? There was an appeal to both.

When we built out our own box, it was made clear by the complexity and dimensionality of the needs we were addressing for our clients that our box could grow and make this shift. But, it did require us to do something fundamentally different from others in our space. We understood to truly create that unique hybrid we would be forced to make fundamentally different decisions to address all four sides of our box. We recognized that we could not address two obvious sides of it—strategy and engagement—alone. Our allocation of resources, especially around talent, became a central focus—prioritizing the hiring of organizational anthropologists and psychologists over account executives and creatives sent shockwaves through the organization and created challenges in how we sold services. Every side of our box was challenged and rethought. While we were ahead of our time with this approach, it is interesting to see how prescient this decision was with major consulting firms like McKinsey and Deloitte acquiring design firms to build capacity and retrofit their operations into this new world. Our ability to see the four sides of our box and to build them out together in a purposeful way allowed us to become our own brand and distinguish ourselves from our competitors.

Evaluating the Effectiveness of Each Side

In our early days of conducting research for clients, we reviewed and sometimes used a number of high-profile surveys available in the marketplace, including culture-specific and employee-engagement surveys. Based on our theory of organizational effectiveness centered around clarity, however, there was not a single survey that would help organizations quickly measure their performance on the key indexes which are critical to fostering clarity. Organizations that focus only on employee engagement, for example, are often missing other important and foundational elements of a high-functioning company. On the other hand, leaders who focus only on strategy and vision are also missing key elements that affect performance. Based on our vast, multidimensional experience across myriad fields and industries, our researchers, social scientists, and business consultants collectively recognized the necessary connections and balance between direction, operations, people, and engagement as crucial. All together, these components were not being carefully measured or analyzed in any of the other surveys on the market. Therefore, we developed a unique, proprietary assessment, the Clarity Performance Index (CPI), which provides an overview of an organization's performance in each of these areas. Ultimately, the Clarity Performance Index measures the extent to which an organization has focused on these key areas and established their foundations to maximize overall performance.

Figure 1.2 provides you with the opportunity to assess and map your company's performance.

CLARITY PERFORMANCE INDEX®

HOW IS YOUR COMPANY PERFORMING?

(Step 1) Carefully read each statement that corresponds to each of the performance dimensions, and rate your company based on the following scale:

1 – strongly disagree; 2 – disagree; 3 – agree; 4 – strongly agree.

DIRECTION

	strongly disagree	disagree	agree	strongly agree
VISION + VALUES: My company has clearly defined values.............	①	②	③	④
STRATEGY: My company has a clear sense of where it is headed...	①	②	③	④
LEADERSHIP: The behaviors of leadership reflect the company's ideal culture..	①	②	③	④

OPERATIONS

ADAPTABILITY: My company adapts well to change.......................	①	②	③	④
PERFORMANCE MANAGEMENT: My company uses clear data metrics to assess performance..	①	②	③	④
SYSTEMS + PROCESSES: The processes and systems put in place by my company help streamline my work..	①	②	③	④

PEOPLE

COACHING + DEVELOPMENT: My company provides consistent, helpful coaching and feedback to each team and individual..	①	②	③	④
TALENT MANAGEMENT: My company has an effective performance evaluation process..	①	②	③	④
TEAM CAPABILITIES: My company encourages collaboration.............	①	②	③	④

ENGAGEMENT

EMPLOYEE CLARITY + FIT: Employees know how their work contributes to company goals..	①	②	③	④
CUSTOMER FOCUS: My company does a great job of engaging with customers..	①	②	③	④
COMMUNICATION EFFECTIVENESS: My company effectively shares information between its parts............................	①	②	③	④

Figure 1.2   Clarity Performance Index

CLARITY PERFORMANCE INDEX®

(Step 2) Using the chart provided, shade in your results for each performance dimension. Example: If you scored your company's strategy a two, you would shade in the first two sections of the strategy triangle.

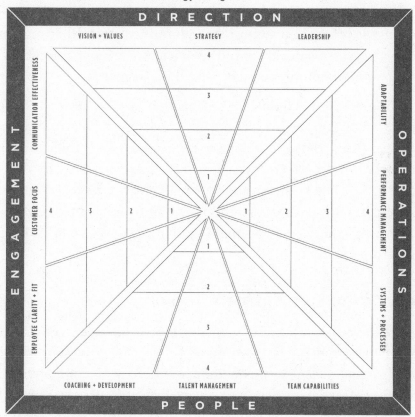

(Step 3) Reflecting on your Clarity Performance Index results, do you see any imbalances within your box? Answer on the lines provided:

_____

_____

_____

_____

_____

_____

45

The Clarity Performance Index is a first step in establishing a baseline for any organization to understand where they currently are. It is also a diagnostic tool to help understand areas of strengths and areas of opportunity. It is an important tool for leaders to have quantitative data to assist in planning and decision making. It is also important to re-administer the CPI at regular intervals to assess progress and to catch any areas that might be falling behind before it affects overall performance.

Some of our clients have seen that when they focus too much on a couple of areas while ignoring other important areas in their company, their scores drop, as does their overall organizational performance. Again, we are looking for purposeful, balanced improvement of all four sides of the box. A company must continually monitor and revisit these areas to ensure that they are continually making progress and moving forward—together.

Four Sides, Two Systems

As we look at the four sides of the box, leaders are constantly trying to search for ways to drive performance in each of the dimensions in each of the quadrants. There is no company that we have worked with that has universally achieved perfect scores in every dimension. In fact, we have yet to have any company with the highest possible score in any one single dimension. Some clients become focused on the numerical values identified in the survey. The score is less important—what is important is how it ranks relative to the other areas. Balance is critical. The organizations that over-index in one area or another often show deficits that correlate to lower-than-expected returns.

We are first focused on clients having a balanced score in each of these areas because each area is needed for an organization to do well. For example, a strong strategy is meaningless without the people and processes needed to achieve an organization's vision and goals. Similarly, smart and talented people cannot be productive as a group without shared vision and values. If an organization's systems and processes are not designed to help employees work effectively, or if an organization does not communicate well with its employees, even the most talented workforce will not be successful at achieving the organization's objectives.

Balance becomes mandatory. We have found that when there is balance between direction and operations, which represents what we have identified as the strategic system and people and engagement, which represents the cultural system, the natural energy in the company is able to flow more organically, driving performance throughout. Overwhelmingly in the research we have conducted, clients have demonstrated that where there is a lack of balance in the systems, there is a lack of organizational performance that correlates directly with the research.

A 2012 *Fast Company* article perfectly captured the need for a balance by stating, "Ultimately, the culture versus strategy question is a false choice. It is like asking whether you would rather back a great poker player with weak cards or an average player with great cards. You're more likely to win when you have both: a great player and great cards. The same goes for culture and strategy. You don't have to choose. Culture doesn't eat strategy, and the company that lets culture do so is likely to starve."

The companies that have stronger strategic systems often have a workforce that is less engaged and less productive. Conversely, companies that have a stronger culture system at the expense of their strategic system have passionate, connected employees who expend energy and resources in ways that do not fully contribute to the company's business objectives.

One of the great examples of the necessary balance of the two systems became obvious as we worked with an international oil and gas exploration and production company. They had become wildly successful due in part to their wildcatter mentality. This entrepreneurial spirit and willingness to take risks served the company well while they were a smaller, more domestically focused operation and during a time when oil climbed steadily toward $100 a barrel. But as the company grew and expanded into international theaters, concerns about the company's commitment to safety grew among the tight-knit oil and gas community. The company believed they had a delicate balance to strike between conforming to best practices established by the "majors" in their business (Exxon, Shell, BP, and so on) while remaining true to their own identity. That identity had unique characteristics that greatly appealed to their employees, many of whom had come over from other, larger oil companies because they were tired of that type of corporate culture. Our work with this company initially focused on populating their box to find innovative ways inside the box to strike this balance. You'll find out a bit about best practices in Chapter 7 on masqueraders. But in this discussion, let's say that we want to populate the box with what is true and enduring for the organization. If there is a reason to adopt practices from an industry standard, your box facilitates a way to commit to that practice while being clear about the impact on your organization. This only happens with purposeful intent. Your box helps you see when an operational issue can affect a value, creating a negative effect with your people as they lose faith in the organization. Everything is connected. With a well-populated box, you can navigate change and be purposeful and in clarity about how each dimension will be affected. You can actually see the wave of change that the impact will bring across the quadrants of the box. Through clarity, we were able to identify ways to be committed to safety and compliant with all regulations while remaining true to the things that defined them and made them successful over time. We were able to elevate safety to the same level as the operational drivers that had always defined the organization. This focus on operational excellence impacted not only safety, but fundamentally recalibrated their approach to business. By populating their box and identifying their four sides, we built out ways to meet their evolving operational needs and create the necessary balance between their strategic and culture systems. This clarity allowed them to grow bigger by thinking small. It also allowed them to shift priorities toward five key imperatives that they saw as crucial toward continuing to grow the business the right way—their way.

Inside the New Normal

The shifting paradigm of going from outside to inside the box takes some getting used to. Leaders worry about losing the innovation and creativity that they previously believed comes from outside-the-box thinking. But, inside-the-box produces more efficiency, more alignment, more purpose, and is a far easier and more effective platform from which to lead. We have always believed that people universally want to support their company and contribute in a positive way. They, like people of all ages and places in life, need structure. They also need and crave definition, connectivity, and a reason to believe. The box provides the structure and the belief system for the company, the leadership, the board, and the workforce. It also provides a tangible thing for all to understand and hold on to. The reality, as our work has proven, is that when everyone is holding on to the same box, they come alive, encourage responsible creativity, and drive real innovation.

CHAPTER 2

The Six Sides of Clarity

The frame of the box that holds the twelve dimensions creating the space where you are in clarity begins to give structure to your work. But, like the world in which we live, nothing is flat. Thus, the next addition is to add dimensionality to the box (Figure 2.1). The organizational box that we have created is actually a cube with four sides, but also with a top and bottom. The fifth and sixth sides of the box add dimension to our box and keep the tasks of the four sides both contained and connected. The dimensionality also provides the place for clarity to reside—right in the center of the box. This is why it is so important to account for all six sides of the box when you plan for performance—it provides the natural home for clarity within your unique organization. The bottom of the box is your foundation, which provides a solid place for the fundamental elements of your organization to firmly rest upon. The top of the box is what opens your organization to the world and takes your company beyond what you do internally—it lifts you with all the promise and dreams of what can be.

THE FIFTH SIDE—FOUNDATION (THE BOTTOM OF THE BOX)

Conventional wisdom might reasonably dictate that you start at the bottom with a firm foundation before building out the sides of your box, and in a perfect business environment it is what leaders would start with right after they have the conceptual framework for their business identified. Unfortunately, businesses don't always have the foresight or time to slow down to think or rethink the foundation of their box, instead relying on the product, service, and the more traditional sides of the flat box. We often hear a groan among leadership teams when we ask them to step back and begin with the foundation because few have discovered, much less practiced an important concept we call strategic patience—this is where leaders invest smartly

DEFINING YOUR BOX

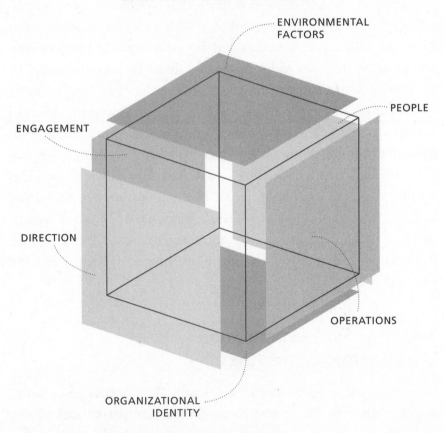

Figure 2.1   Defining Your Box

PART 1: WHAT'S OUTSIDE YOUR BOX?

What external, environmental factors affect or shape who we are?

_____

_____

What do competitors do that we would never identify with or do ourselves?

_____

_____

What regulations or laws are in place that change what we can do?

_____

_____

What market or consumer trends are at odds with our company's current direction?

_____

_____

PART 2: WHAT'S FOUNDATIONAL TO YOUR BOX?

After revealing what you are not, define your organization's identity by answering the following questions:

What are your organization's core characteristics (who are we)?

_____

_____

What is your organization's purpose (why do we exist)?

_____

_____

What are your organization's core values (what motivates us)?

_____

_____

in what they know is important for their business and allow the investment, in time, strategy, or capital, the opportunity to work. Instead, they circumvent the process and want to get to the things that they have perceived matters most to them or excites their desire to make something happen immediately. Long-term success and sustainability is not about being the first; it is about being the most intentional and thoughtful.

Obviously, anyone who owns a house knows that your foundation is paramount. When ready to buy or sell your house, you are most excited about and want to focus on decorating or staging, or perhaps opening up your floor plan to make the rooms look bigger. Very few of us want to focus on the foundation even though it is what will bring the stability and support to all of the other things you want to happen and experience in the space above it. You take great pleasure in creating the space *within*. It is so easy to picture yourself in that beautiful home. However, the moment we discover a home we're interested in buying or our home we're trying to sell has a foundation or structural problem, all the sirens go off and the red flags are thrown. That juicy budget that was going to give you pristine hardwood floors in the entryway suddenly gets appropriated to the foundation that no one sees, but is fundamental to the long-term viability of the home. And it is expensive. You are expending resources without getting the benefit of being able to see it or touch it. But you know that without a sturdy and stable foundation, nothing else in your home can take place without great caution and risk. Your foundation grounds you and keeps your structure firmly in place while creating the spaces in which you live and work. Without the foundation, none of the visible parts of your home can exist.

Luckily for us, making sure an organization's foundation is established in business is actually exciting and thought provoking, for both established companies as well as those in their early stages. Leaders begin to understand that solidifying the base is not only a foundational, no pun intended, exercise; it is critical to the ultimate success of your business.

Our fifth side of the box starts with identity.

Identity: Who We Are, Why We Exist, and What Motivates Us

Organizational identity is the enduring essence of an organization, the unique product of its history. What was true about this organization 10 years ago? What is true today? What needs to be true 10 years from now? Identity is not something that can be copied from others and it serves as the anchor that grounds an organization and acts as the filter through which it screens its actions.

Over the years, we've looked at many elements that make up identity but have narrowed it down to just four that are impactful: *characteristics*, *purpose*, *values*, and *traditions*.

Characteristics are what is central, enduring, and distinct about the organization. It is what is perceived by employees, regardless of changes encountered, as the anchor they can hold on to and rely upon. It is what gives the company life and a connection over time.

An organization's characteristics answer the question: Who are we?

Some examples from a research-based health institute that we worked with include:

- Devotion to cutting-edge research
- Leading the field
- Inspiring pioneering procedures

Purpose is why an organization exists. It is the glue that binds people together in common cause, answering the question: Why do we do what we do? What needs do we fill? What impact do we have?

Some examples from a leading museum intent on clarifying its purpose include:

- Preserving the history and artifacts of something valued
- Teaching others how to communicate more effectively
- Planning solid financial futures that fuel the dreams of others
- Challenging participants to get involved in our community
- Inspiring others to not be a bystander but an upstander

Values are the motivators. Values are the beliefs and motives that leaders and employees hold in common. Values unite people through a shared sense of direction and motivation.

Some examples of values from our own company include:

- Embrace and lead change
- Think like an entrepreneur
- Create collaboratively
- Design for impact
- Love what we do and it shows

Traditions are the beliefs, behaviors, and activities that have been passed down within the organization that set it apart from others and help foster a sense of shared identity. In organizations, there are the big *T*'s, which are the traditions that cannot be messed with, and the little *t*'s that are the newer traditions that organizations have the opportunity to mold and reshape over time.

Some examples of traditions that we see in companies include:

- Company family picnic or crawfish boil
- Company holiday party

- Exploration or learning days (where companies or departments visit other businesses or attractions)

- Special recognition programs

- Being connected or giving to a certain charity organization

While companies work to establish and clearly articulate their foundation, they often don't see it come into play or truly understand its value until the organization faces a challenge or crisis. Our consultants had the opportunity to work with one of the premier schools in the country when the institution became embroiled in a crisis brought on by a series of disagreements and misunderstandings. It centered around the perceived social contract between the institution and the parents, faculty and staff, and students. Each of the constituents had their own definition of the school's culture, because the school had not defined it in its own words. The school, at first, tried to communicate its way out of its predicament with a series of email communications. Unfortunately, because of a lack of depth and real connection to the issue at hand, the email communications only exacerbated the situation. The school interviewed multiple consulting groups, planning to conduct a survey. Each consulting firm being considered was asked to construct a recommended approach to crafting a survey that would give insight into the explosive issues in question. Instead, we approached the situation with a more holistic, organizational identity focus, understanding that particular incident not as a singular issue but as a systemic symptom taking form. What needed to be explored were the core understandings and beliefs that they held and embraced, for those were what would direct any and every social contract, perceived or stated. When we were able to comprehend and bring in their perceptions of what was distinct about the organization, what they valued, and what the key characteristics were that defined the organization, the school was able to clearly frame its social contract. Once their actual social contract was in place, it allowed the community to be heard and come together. This forced disparate voices among the constituents to be minimized and ultimately led them to decide whether they could opt in or out of the defined environment. The foundational work resonated with each of the constituent groups, previously inflamed over vagaries and misperceptions. It ensured space for the unique perspective each group brought. By seeing that they were valued and heard, each was willing to accept the differences and embrace the stated social contract, resulting in increased performance of 30 percent year after year for three consecutive years following the blowup. As much as the client can point to the performance growth as being the metric of which they are most proud, it is actually the work to identify the bottom of their box that is their most profound and lasting achievement. If asked, parents or faculty in their community could not quantify the performance success, nor even today would they remember it. However, what they do know is that things just feel right—and that is because they are in synch with and connected to the bottom of the box—with clearly defined characteristics, purpose, values, and traditions their leaders created.

THE SIXTH SIDE: ENVIRONMENT (THE TOP OF THE BOX)

As we define organizational identity being made up of four elements (characteristics, purpose, values, and traditions), there are also three key elements that make up the environmental side, the top of our box. This side encourages us to ask three broad questions to get a sense of how our characteristics, purpose, and values align with the outside world. When we define our organizational identity, we must then ask: What are our stakeholders saying, what are our stakeholders doing, and how are our stakeholders feeling? These three elements make up the external yin to our internal yang.

The strategy dimension of the box certainly considers the analysis of the outside environment. Classic tools like SWOT analysis, PESTLE analysis, five-forces diagram, and market research can help us make sense of the market around us and better understand what our customers value. The sixth side, the top of the box, encourages a higher-level approach. It causes us to account for and adapt to the changing market trends and industrial forces that influence our company, making our company more adaptable and resilient in the process.

What people say, how they act, and what they are really feeling is not always clear or completely in alignment with our internal culture. In contract negotiations, we may be dealing with someone on the other side of the table who says they care about relationships and hold values like integrity in the highest esteem. But when the going gets tough, will they live their espoused values? Will they follow through on their commitments if their business hits a hard patch? Can you trust what people are saying without a proper accounting of their recent actions and the nature of what is going on around their business?

With Houston as my hometown, I witnessed firsthand how the rise and fall of Enron had a major impact on our community. There were warning signs from within the company, and outside on Wall Street, but few people heeded these signals. Instead, thousands of people took Enron at their espoused core values: communication, respect, integrity, and excellence. People were willing to believe what they were being told. Hindsight is always 20/20 and it took tremendous courage for the whistleblowers to finally stand up, but it is a lesson to be learned for all employees and stakeholders going forward. What people say may not align with what they are doing and certainly not what they are really thinking. Far too often, people use communication as a veil to cover up the decisions going on beneath the surface or in an attempt to persuade others of their righteousness.

In activating our sixth side of the box, be sure to ask what are our customers saying about us? How would they characterize our company? What would they say is central, enduring, or distinct about us?

Our purpose defines why we exist and describes what we do. The second question we must ask in the environment is what are our customers doing? Are there trends or fads in the market that are affecting consumer behavior? Are these, in fact, trends or could they be a signal of a substitute to our product or service?

On the surface, these questions might feel obvious. In fact, these very questions may be what got you into your business to begin with. Business leaders are constantly surveying customer behavior to ensure that their actions align with their company's stated purpose. When there is alignment, there is a need being met by a service. But over time, these questions are often asked less and less frequently because of unintentional habits that form and mediocrity sets in. But in a purposeful organization, one should always check in and ask, "Is my purpose still relevant in today's marketplace?" The horse-and-buggy salesmen, telephone operators, and video rental retailers of yesteryear should serve as reminders that nothing is permanent and every purpose must be questioned from time to time ... and sooner than you might think.

Our team has had the privilege to work with a community icon, a revered museum, steeped in tradition and history. The organization has successfully navigated the changes in the environment and the shifts in the interests of their constituents.

Only in the past several years has the organization begun to spread its reach outside the very traditional framework its founders envisioned. The founders created an atmosphere that protected the past at all costs, never realizing the changes in our world that could possibly necessitate a shift or expansion of the museum and its powerful lessons. But, faced with dwindling attendance, a shrinking philanthropic base, and an uncertain future because of the changing interests of the next generations, the museum was challenged to do what was never envisioned—change with the times. This led to contentious dialog and stiffening positions—all by people who cared passionately for the same cause and place. Basic conversations were misconstrued. Words were twisted and meanings changed—all by honest people who simply shared different perspectives. Some were afraid to change and others were afraid of not changing. Yet, at the core, they cared about the survival of the place they all loved. Only when each member of the expanded board was able to express him- or herself individually (through a card sorting methodology in which each member could identify his/her most important foundational beliefs and then plot them on a chart creating a mode of responses), was clarity evident. While they could not voice their agreement verbally, the mode on the walls demonstrated a shared belief in the foundational elements that defined the museum. While the older generation seemed to propose a strict, narrow interpretation of the mission and the younger generation a more liberal approach, in actuality, there was strong agreement on the purpose and organizational characteristics that allowed the museum's leadership to effectively define, and in some cases, expand what the museum was all about. The old and new finally heard each other, or at least, was willing to listen to the other side. The ultimate result—strong agreement; slightly, yet purposefully expanded box; defined, clear identity; and record philanthropic support leading to a future that will serve both the old and the new. They finally understood that their unwillingness to fully grasp and address their changing environment was jeopardizing the future they were so fiercely trying to protect. The work they did on the top and bottom of their box ensured a future that was relevant not only to their founders, but to the next generation and subsequent generations that will follow.

Finally, the last question requires keen intuition, or what many describe as emotional intelligence. We should always be mindful of what those around us are feeling at any given moment. As stated earlier, the things people say may not be what they mean, but this doesn't have to be indicative of malicious intent. Many times, people say what they perceive you want to hear, don't let their guard down, or express shortened versions of the ideas they intend to convey. It is important to ask yourself if the story you are being told is one of convenience or the reality of the situation. When it comes to interpreting communications from others, one way to dive deeper into the full reality of what they're saying is by empathizing with the feelings and intentions beneath the veil of language they use. What is the mood in our pool of stakeholders? How is the news, the social climate, or the political landscape skewing the attitudes of the environment around us? A keen sense of the prevailing sentiment around us that is authentic, and not just what is spoken, will give further clarity as you round your sense of the environmental factors that can push against your six-sided box. As your purpose and identity from the bottom of the box feeds and gives foundation to the four walls of the box, this top of the box filters in all that is external. When creating the top of your box, the onus falls on your company to create a connective membrane that is flexible enough to adapt and permeable enough to allow the range of insight in. The top of the box also opens us to the world and exposes us to the external forces that are constantly changing in our environment.

Where Are We Going and How Are We Getting There?

Much has been written about strategy and its importance in shaping an organization's future and delivering return to shareholders. Similar to how our values are shared both as foundation and as a dimension, strategy is an essential partner when considering environment, as the forces pushing on our box from the outside encourage us to make changes and redefine value for our customers. Through the integration of environment and strategy, you can better identify your competitive advantage, navigate change, and more effectively push the boundaries of performance.

While identity and purpose anchor our organizations, strategy takes us boldly out into the world. It helps us brace for change but also to make change our ally. Interpreting change is a crucial function of the top of the box and critical for those companies looking to grow, explore new services or industries, or protect themselves from volatility in the marketplace. While many want to ascribe a more undesirable definition to change and what it can represent to the workforce, we simply view it as a reality in the world in which we live today.

Much of our work has involved companies that come together through merger, acquisition, and even hostile takeovers. When the companies combine, they often do not initially achieve the financial results that were expected by their investors, shareholders, or leaders. In virtually each situation, at the root of their performance issue was a lack of clarity by way of a dueling culture that was inconsistent, reactive, and unconnected. Companies are so focused on the operational complexities of merging the companies, that they delay the cultural component that is often what determines the multiple for success. One of the most successful acquisition strategies we have worked with was implemented by a start-up company committed to culture and organizational identity at their inception. Instead of combining companies operationally and then redefining the culture years later, this visionary company in the energy space took a highly proactive approach to culture by investing in organizational identity, values, and behaviors at the start. They did not wait to begin the acquisition strategy and then define culture. They understood that when they looked at the environment and competitive landscape, this clarity of purpose and values could be their competitive advantage. Instead of waiting for it to manifest, they aggressively and proactively designed it far ahead of the operational platform being implemented. It was the definition of the culture they wished to create that helped determine the acquisitions and ultimately the integration strategy. With each company they acquired, not only did they work to understand and integrate that company's closely held beliefs, they also set a clear expectation of their own beliefs. By addressing the four sides of the box and the dimensionality from the start, the company was able to norm each of the acquired companies to the whole of the organization faster and more efficiently than originally projected. More importantly, the new companies were able to hold on to and embrace their new organization from the start. This clarity and purposeful dimensionality increased profitability months earlier than the stated, and ambitious, projections. When mergers take place, the acquired company's tradition and former vitality often become suppressed by the force of the dominant culture. This approach, however, hardly ever works smoothly, and somewhere down the road, performance issues and workplace tension will result. In this case, the box provided them an arena to proactively build the organization that could effectively and uniquely compete in the space—starting day one.

ENVIRONMENT: WHAT GOES ON AROUND US

External forces all around us affect our clarity and can have an entropic effect if unrecognized or left unchecked. As the environment filters in from the outside, being aware of and planning for shifts in competitive forces, government regulations, industry constraints, and so on allows for a business to nimbly shift focus and respond to dynamic change more successfully than those without such clarity. *Clarity becomes both interpreter and incubator of how the outside forces will affect our internal climate of culture.* We instill stability in the businesses with the expectations set in the other five sides, which have a greater impact on our destiny than the environment alone. Expectations are important in understanding the sixth side. As we introduced earlier, we cannot get away from our fundamental belief that organizations and individuals are products of their expectations, not their environments. But, that does not negate the power and importance of the environment and the factors that drive it. If organizations are aptly understanding their environment and accounting for future shifts before they fully take place, they have the chance of being at the forefront of the industry by exceeding the consumers' expectations.

In clarity, we realize that the environment is rich with resources and opportunity for us, not just chaotic factors beyond our control. We recognize that while they may belong to someone else, they are still there for us to know and understand.

We also look at the environment and mindset of the internal organization. We recognize that it becomes a critical part of our ability to see the totality of the environment. As we have shared, when leaders understand at a fundamental level and embrace what is central, enduring, and distinctive about the organization and are able to effectively convey that to their employees, they can work with shared passion to encourage and ultimately achieve alignment. One of the factors that is important to living up to all sides of the box is the mindset of the entirety of the workforce. A 2012 study on strategic environmental scanning and organizational performance confirms this notion, stating how management needs to take into cognizance the environment's dynamism and uncertainty when adopting any strategy. The study revealed the significant relationship that exists between strategic environmental scanning and organizational performance, signifying the necessary role scanning has in creating an effective, proactively responding organization.

No one likes a Pollyanna; but at Deutser, we believe that finding the positive side is what separates great companies and leaders from merely good ones. We believe that embedding positivity into the DNA of an organization creates the foundation for longevity and the expectation of greatness. In fact, positivity and optimism are key measures in our assessments and surveys. What makes a positive culture? Leaders in touch with their people, people aligned with the organizational expectations, and people who are openly encouraged to share their insights and build a belief in what they have set up, by way of their box, and what they can collectively achieve.

Understanding and accepting both the role and importance of positivity in the psyche of an organization is a fundamental part of leading. Because of the constant bombardment of information that confronts us daily, leaders can easily succumb to information overload. If we are not careful, these distractions will derail us. To counter this, we employ a weekly exercise to ensure that, as we think about our box and the environment in which it exists, we are purposefully leaving behind things that don't serve us while caring for things that help us and reinforcing the positivity that defines us when we're at our best.

PURPOSEFUL POSITIVITY
A Weekly Exercise

Gratitude for all we accomplish every day is the foundation for positivity and performance. Yet, as each new week begins, leaders often hold on to shortcomings, frustrations, and negativity that they encountered over the past week, quarter, or year. Research shows that when we let go of the past, good and bad, we are able to achieve a level of clarity to move forward with purpose. Please take the time to complete this worksheet to help put last week behind you and prepare for what is next, and next after next.

Letting go of what I need to leave behind.

What are those things that did not go well or created negativity or resentment that you continue to hold on to at your company's or your detriment?

1. _____
2. _____
3. _____

Identifying what we must take forward.

What are those things that, when completed, will bring positive value to you and your organization? These are tasks, projects, or obstacles that must be addressed.

1. _____
2. _____
3. _____
4. _____
5. _____

Figure 2.2   Purposeful Positivity

Expressing gratitude for all that we have accomplished.

There is nothing more important than identifying the good that we achieve each and every week. It is easy for us to allow negativity to form clouds of doubt or discomfort. For your well-being, it is crucial to identify and express gratitude for the good, positive things we created or are a part of. List 10 specific things you're grateful for here.

1. _____

2. _____

3. _____

4. _____

5. _____

6. _____

7. _____

8. _____

9. _____

10. _____

As I reflect on environmental challenges, I think about a situation where I fundamentally misread the environment and the factors driving our client's decision making. I was faced with one of the most professionally and personally challenging situations when a long-time client was forced to deal with a devastating community event of historic proportions. Everywhere I looked there were messages of compassion and genuine concern. With few exceptions, this was a moment of unmistakable human triumph. The community fiercely rallied around recovery with companies forgoing credit to simply do what was right and to best take care of people and the city they called home. Everything in the environment seemed so crystal clear—especially the way people of different ethnic and socioeconomic backgrounds came together to support each other.

This was one of the few times that there were no competing environmental factors to cloud what was happening. Yet, the conflict for me came when one of my oldest, most revered clients went silent and removed itself from the community support net. The company that had quietly always done the right thing, out of the spotlight, remained on the sidelines. I was personally devastated and confused. How could this happen? How could the company I have carefully guided over years of work desert not only me and my value system, but our community? I began to wonder if I had been wrong about our values being aligned. I took this as a personal affront. I asked my team, and the client, how could anyone be so tone deaf to the cries of the community and those in need? I never got an answer. I knew I was right. But, was I? Was the client tone deaf? Or, was it me, and those closest to me, who were blinded? I learned that the leader was far from tone deaf. True, he wasn't listening to the community. It was moving in ways few could understand, unless they were part of the tragic events. But he was listening to his board and the leaders to whom he reported. He was doing exactly what was expected of him—focusing on the business, not the community. In the end, it was I who was blind to the dimensionality of business and the competing factors for which all leaders must account. Dimensionality speaks to the complexity that outsiders often understand and we sometimes miss as leaders. In clarity, you must take into account the full environment and all sides of the box.

THE CONNECTION OF IDENTITY AND ENVIRONMENT

When there is clarity of the top and bottom of the box, we often find the unmistakable driver to culture. Most organizations overlook or don't fully grasp the impact of culture on performance. In clarity, one of our primary objectives is to help leaders understand their culture for what it is and to be able to identify what they want it to be while working to fiercely protect what must never change. Most consultants focus on identifying a slew of problems and then working to correct them. In using our process, leaders are able to emphasize positivity and focus on *what is* while setting expectations of *what can be*. That is why we start with the box. When we return to our shared identity, values, and traditions, it helps us connect through what is shared and similar rather than disconnect through what is different and troublesome. Some might scoff at positive psychology and the power of positive thinking, but I have seen how authentic positivity holds the box together and plays a vital role in aligning and strengthening an organization's culture. In fact, at Deutser, we insist on it or we really can't help the organization. Organizations that find ways to emphasize a positive outlook and attitude in the workplace are more likely to see improved performance and motivation among employees. Strong leadership is more than having a charismatic head of the organization. Yes, a strong leader is where it starts, but great leadership, in clarity, has the opportunity to inspire at a level that cascades across the whole of the organization in order to embolden, motivate, and steer toward even greater success.

One of the great learning opportunities for me as a leader of clarity and culture came when I was asked to plan a retreat for 50 CEOs and their spouses. I was assigned the city of Las Vegas—the most unlikely venue for me, as I am not a big gambler or partier. My directive came with a twist in that it could not be the Vegas that any of the successful CEOs had ever experienced. On one of my eight scouting trips there, I experienced a fundamentally different environment. I had the opportunity to go behind the scenes, deep inside the operations of some of Las Vegas's best-known and successful hotels, casinos, and theatrical performance venues. It reinforced the insight that one Cirque du Soleil show is not like any other—each show is unique with a uniquely, purposefully designed environment and identity. The same is true for the casinos and hotels—from deep beneath the bowels of the operations, the identity is absolutely focused. The more successful operations built a purposeful culture around that identity. One went so far as to create an experience for the employees that rivaled what it provided for its guests—with free meals prepared specially for employees by the chefs of the hotel, organic gardens grown specifically for employee meals, unlimited amenities, employee-focused recognition and rewards, and an environment that ensured the comfort of its workforce while they took a break from the stimulation required when interacting with guests. Rival casinos did some of the same things, but they outsourced the food to presumably save money, which signaled, intentionally or unintentionally, that those employees were not valued the same as by other hotels. Interestingly, the hotel/casino that went the furthest in trying to live up to its identity, installed high-grade, extra-plush carpet to comfort employees who, while on their feet all day, could finally find full comfort during break time. Even though the ultra-plush carpet might bring comfort to tired legs and ankles, their good intentions failed to account for the extra difficulty it caused for the men and women pushing heavy carts up ramps and across large pathways. Finally, the leadership recognized the challenge and changed the environment, but held true to the very identity it lives up to each day, from employees to guests to visitors. Identity matters and it translates to the way that everyone who touches your company is cared for and valued.

Organizations are formed with the best intentions—with thoughtful consideration of passion, long-term viability, and compatibility. But the research is clear: A sound strategy is simply not enough to guarantee future success. While there is no one-size-fits-all approach, the more leaders focus their attention on being clear with the desired culture and positive outlook, the better positioned their organizations will be to weather economic downturns, thrive during uncertain times, and grow with confidence and clarity.

Recognition by leaders that every organization has a culture ultimately begs further examination into whether it is a high-performing one. Is it purposeful or accidental? Southwest Airlines and Apple have very purposeful cultures. Some could argue that some habitually poor-performing sports franchises—you can fill in myriad names—have cultures that are the antithesis of purposeful. Action after action demonstrates the lack of clarity from the inside out, leading to an accidental culture: one that exists, but not in a way that will help drive culture or performance. There is a major disconnect. Organizations that once were purposeful can also experience a gradual slippage away from the previous purposeful intentions, shifting it off course and going somewhere you don't want it to go as an accidental culture. Part of bringing clarity into an organization is to create or return an organization to a purposeful culture in which the existing culture is clearly articulated and clear parameters are given to protect it. In this culture-sustaining process, vision, ideas, and actions are developed regarding how to grow it, steadily and surely with intention. Within this journey are clearly articulated strategic imperatives that act as guideposts for all employees who can be evaluated to determine if your team is on course. When this is firmly in place, the top and bottom of the box brings unrivaled opportunity. Your positive culture will align to enable you to actualize the highest level of performance and progress possible.

This is especially poignant to me. My career started in a most unusual environment—one of the oldest, most acclaimed circuses, Ringling Bros. and Barnum & Bailey Circus. It was an environment that took great pride in the past and held on to history more than any organization that I have worked with over the past three-plus decades. Not only did they value the history of this particular circus, but they were also steeped in a societal culture that spanned generations. For much of its nearly 150-plus year history, the circus's box was incredibly well-defined with little chance or need for deviation. Their unwavering identity was the strength of the organization and they executed it nearly flawlessly. Unfortunately, the world was changing around them at a much faster pace than they could, or were willing to, change. They didn't focus on the environmental side and failed to address the many technological and social changes that were accelerating and invading the safe world that they had created. After all, part of the allure of the circus was to create a place that felt like a visit to another era, and the value of nostalgia gave way to delights elsewhere. They began to fade out of the psyche of the American consumer. When they attempted to modernize and conform to new, changing societal norms, they lost their base and their way. Their box was purposefully—and for many years, successfully—designed on a small scale to accommodate very specific parameters. Yet, they were unwilling to look at the totality of the box and never connected with the environmental side or took into account the world around them. They did not recognize this early enough or with enough vigor. Ultimately, the company failed. The lesson is that no matter the clarity around the four sides of the box, the lack of understanding and appreciation for the organization's identity, and the acceptance of the dimensionality and environmental elements in which the box resides, will ultimately dismantle even a good product. The box cannot be left on the shelf to collect dust once it is constructed. Change is the constant environment within which clarity exists. So, the box must continue to be evaluated and updated, taking into consideration all six of its sides.

This is as true to a 150-year-old company as it is to our company. When our company finally decided to think inside the box and defined the type of business we were in and where we wanted to go, we had to take a hard look in the mirror and define what the Deutser organization was. Only when we looked at our identity did we realize we were not connected at the core. In fact, there was very little that connected us, except for our passion for solving problems and our belief in positive psychology. We were producing work that was transformational and far exceeded the expectation of our clients, yet the process and dysfunction internally challenged our existence. Too often, we were disconnected, working against ourselves and inhibiting our own growth. We realized some of our people were wrong for the strategy we had identified, and the company had misaligned values. We understood why some people were so successful in our environment and others were less effective. We recognized that everything in business, at least in our world, is connected and requires a complexity of solution that is multifaceted. We knew that as we were constructed at the time we could create only so much impact. We also understood that, in addition to the "person," we needed to find unique talents and skillsets. After we established our core values, purpose statements, and characteristics, we went to work building a team with the diverse skills and backgrounds required for us to be a consulting firm that had unique expertise in navigating ambiguity and achieving clarity for and with clients. It required us to not hire traditional consultants, as they brought a different philosophical framework and were less successful dealing with the ambiguity, chaos, and creativity that is inherent in our company. So we went on a hiring spree, hiring organizational anthropologists, industrial psychologists, executive coaches, MBAs, a PhD, designers, writers, digital experts, artists, as well as community engagement and media experts. We even tinkered with a minister to help our clients navigate crises. The dimensionality of our people and the uniqueness of their experiences brings a wealth of perspective to a client to help address the most complex issues with which single-issue firms often struggle or choose less far-reaching metrics to define success. It is this unconventional, holistic approach to people, connected by positive psychology, that allows us to be true to who we are and to deliver a different level of solution and creativity. We finally became what we had always preached we were—and it took the dimensionality of the box to help us finally get there.

The box, like your leadership, must be purposeful. The foundation you set is fundamental to your ability to manipulate and maneuver within the box. To many leaders, going back to basics seems like a waste of time, effort, and resources. That is, only until they do it and experience the magnitude of the power and connection it creates for the leadership team and the organization. Whether it is a start-up, a nonprofit, a 100-year-old thriving business, or publicly traded company, there is immense value in going back to the identity and understanding the environmental factors that will ultimately shape your future. You may not be able to control the factors around you, but you can and must be aware, react, prepare for them, and anticipate what will happen next, and more importantly, next after next. Your box is defined. Now you have what you need to move forward and drive the performance you desire.

CHAPTER 3

Misalignment Will Derail You

There's no better time to be in business. Just a generation ago, if a start-up eventually grew to be valued at $100 million, it would have most likely required several MBAs, at least 20 years of hard work, grit, and perseverance, a minimum of a few dozen employees, the right timing, and a generous amount of luck. However, in 2018, graduate business schools are having a hard time filling their classrooms, teenagers are writing code in lieu of college essays, and venture capitalists are pouring money into start-ups—some of which are valued at $100 million only months after closing their funding rounds.

Talk of the bubble aside, the reality is that the trend of savvy entrepreneurs and spirited investors searching for the next big thing will continue. And of course, this will only grow the digital economy and advance innovations in how we communicate. But with these constant changes disrupting the way people access and share information in an already interconnected, always-on world, it has become increasingly difficult for leaders, regardless of industry, to keep up, adapt, and grow with confidence. When we are in clarity, we both understand and accept that change is a constant state, but the rapid rate of change today compels us to reexamine the way we think about the world, along with how we react and plan for it.

As a result, organizations are now facing a new reality: There is no more uncertain or challenging time to be in business. And, without clarity, there is no roadmap to effectively and consistently achieve success.

Consider a major retail company whose stock price was singlehandedly driven down by a disgruntled customer's online comments. Or a storied, consistently top-ranked NCAA football program, known for its excellence both on and off the field, that, seemingly overnight through a series of grossly mishandled campus issues, had its reputation tarnished and future placed in doubt. Or, think about the respected oil company that experienced a pattern of work-related injuries to its employees that thrust it onto the brink of bankruptcy.

Each organization faced its own clarity conundrum, and while these situations may seem unrelated, they are strikingly similar. Each situation could have been avoided. These companies failed to adhere to some of the most basic principles of clarity. They didn't stay true to who they were, they lacked focus on their strategic goals, their attention to tending the environment was weak or absent, and they prioritized sales over safety and growth. In other words, they were out of alignment with their box. They lacked organizational clarity. So how could these companies have avoided these mistakes? It starts with three questions: Why do we exist? What needs do we fill? Why do we do what we do?

The logic behind this is simple, and it certainly isn't brain surgery. But it is a science. Our work and research underscore the importance of not just answering these three questions, but focusing on how and when these questions are asked and answered, and who is asking and answering them. These questions are at the core of recognizing misalignments that affect culture, strategy, and even an organization's existence. Why is uncertainty so closely linked to misalignment? Because misalignment is the weak link in your structure that stresses the whole of your organization and creates an workplace ripe for chaos, disagreement, and dissention. Misalignment keeps organizations from actualizing their purpose because the flow is off and additional effort and resources are required simply to get things back on track, much less move them forward. Misalignment creates distraction, especially in the people quadrant, as we get caught up in things that mutate and spread in unpredictable and unwelcomed ways rather than the energy flowing up naturally through the culture and environment.

By no means are these three questions a guarantee for improved performance. But they do help to jumpstart the process and direct you to a potential pathway to being in clarity. You've already considered these questions as you built your six-sided box, but they are again called out in this discussion because they provide triage when you know something is off and want to attend to it. But, they require a leader to stop, to ask the questions and to address them. Unfortunately, in the haste to hire the right people, build the best product, and generate the most revenue, many leaders are either too focused on the immediate task at hand or issue of the day or too overworked and preoccupied to stop and take an inside-out view of their company to determine (and often discover) how misaligned they really are. A recent *Harvard Business Review* article lists four main reasons for misaligned enterprises: Leaders are unaware of the risks associated with misalignment, nobody takes ownership of the alignment process, complexity makes alignment that much harder, and activity gets mistaken for progress. "In essence, misalignment is a systemic issue that is often out of sight, hiding behind the surface-level problems which people try to cover with a Band-Aid or remove. Too often, the effects that arise from misalignment are perceived as the causes themselves, and the real source of misalignment remains untouched." Getting rid of a few bad apples in an organization, while it may be beneficial, is often not the larger, more lasting solution—since they may have been created from a much more systemic problem within the company. Rebranding as a means to a fresh start is not always the best long-term option. We all know that there are many great-looking companies whose outward perceptions belie their dysfunctional inner workings and culture. And in the age of Yelp, Glassdoor, and Snapchat, it won't be long before the world exposes that contrast.

Also, regardless of how much your revenues have increased, how high your stock has risen, or how productive your workforce is, a profitable organization is not always an aligned organization. Just because your organization is aligned doesn't necessarily mean you will be profitable. But if you commit to the process and state of being in clarity, you'll have a much better shot at recognizing misalignments before they spread and send energy and resources in directions that are off plan or even completely outside your box. The ability to recognize misalignments protects your company and aids in building a unique organization with a solid foundation that can thrive for generations. You may not have the valuation of the next big social media start-up, but you'll have a decent shot at outlasting them.

You may be asking why we're approaching this as misalignment instead of putting our efforts into alignment. Clarity itself clears the way to a more natural progression to alignment. Here we want to sound the call to extract misalignments or at least identify them so that you begin to adjust the appropriate quadrants in the box. (See Figure 3.1) Misalignment occurs throughout the organization, at different times and in many varieties. Some can be easily addressed; others are symptomatic of something more serious that requires a different type of intervention. In either case, the misalignment cannot be left to rot from the inside; it must be addressed.

IS YOUR ORGANIZATION ALIGNED?

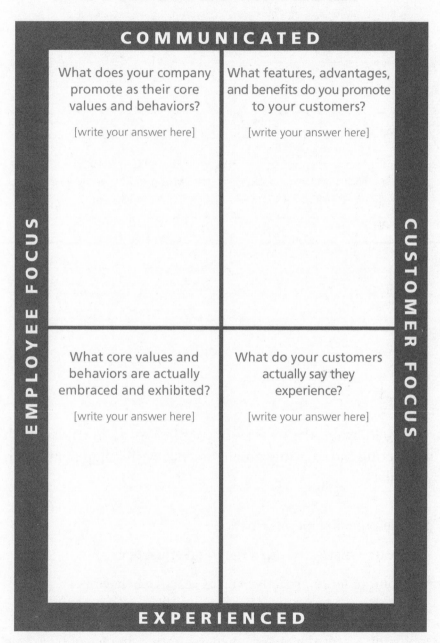

Figure 3.1   Is Your Organization Aligned

FOLLOW-UP QUESTIONS

Based on your answers, how much misalignment is there between what your organization communicates and what is actually experienced on the outside? Why?

_____

_____

_____

_____

_____

How much alignment or misalignment is there between who we say we are internally and who we tell our customers we are externally? Why?

_____

_____

_____

_____

_____

Building out the six sides of your box works in tandem with uncovering and adjusting misalignments. As misalignments clear, you will:

- Open the flow of information

- Create synergy, transparency, and efficiency

- Promote more proactive versus reactive behaviors

- Remove bottlenecks and waiting

- Create a sense of shared ownership (moving away from one person feeling alone in shouldering the responsibility)

- Improve the quality of work

- Drive higher performance outcomes

Let's look at some common misalignments.

Vision vs. Execution

One of my favorite walls in our office is our back wall. It had a simple message: The only lines we care about are our clients' growing bottom lines. Under the message was a clever red shelf lined with trophies and a small line of text that read: A little recognition from our industry and peers is nice as well. It was simply the last stop on a purposeful storytelling mission through our innovative space. We proudly tour hundreds of executives through our space and each one gravitated to random areas in the office. Except one CEO who became outraged by the message on the back wall. I asked him what was so upsetting? He said, "It's not the message. It's the fact that the message makes me think you don't get it. Your words and actions demonstrate a level of misalignment that is concerning." Surprised, I asked him what he meant. He continued, "If you think it's all about the bottom line for me, as a CEO, you either don't understand the CEO or you are working for the wrong ones." He paused and then said, "All that matters to me is that your work saves lives every day, that you are preventing suicides, that you are able to support our environment that is inclusive and values employees. Those things drive our bottom line and they are what matter." Needless to say, when a thoughtful, highly respected client believes that your thinking is out of line with his, you have unveiled a critical misalignment that needs your immediate attention. Not only did we quickly create a new concept for the back wall and execute it immediately, we took that thinking back into our own box and made sure that this misalignment was checked throughout the box for any thinking that had spilled over into our clarity.

Status Quo vs. Moving Forward

The concept of "good kills" is one that we originally used in context in conversations focused on companies and their attitudes toward safety. The idea we tried to convey was that good enough proved over and over to be one of the reasons accident rates continued to climb within certain industries. They proved that good wasn't really good, and that good actually did kill. But, we found that this concept is even more prevalent in businesses across a variety of industries. Why? Because good kills, not necessarily people, but organizations and their ability to grow. Good is the engine for status quo. We have worked with high-performing companies that suddenly stall. After presenting research to a company, one president asked, "How is it possible for our numbers to drop so dramatically in a year?" The answer was simple—the company was so focused on all the factors outside of the business, including a challenging economic environment, that they lost sight of the need to elevate the entirety of their business, not simply one part. To them, because the business was operating at a "good or very good" level, they were able to move their attention from the very things they could control and support, especially their people, who were operating in a high-pressure, high-stakes business, which demanded accuracy. Because they had always navigated through challenging times, with great, responsible leaders, they knew that by maintaining their focus "where it had always been," it would help them get through the challenges and maintain their leadership position. The misalignment of taking their focus off what was going on within the company and placing it in on what was outside of their control had a cascading effect that touched every aspect of the company, including the bottom line. When the leader recognized the misalignment, he did what great leaders do—he took action.

Communication vs. Intention

When the people on the front lines are left to interpret the words and intent of the leadership, it creates gaps in understanding and action, causing misalignment. In working on the culture of an international company with offices in the United States, South America, Egypt, Australia, and the United Kingdom, we helped navigate a challenging situation after the company republished its core values across the world to all employees. Before this republication, their values were pushed only in the United States. They thought it would be a good idea to "share this in the spirit of transparency and communication." But they weren't looking at the dynamics of the full box. They had missed the people component of cultural differences and this action led to great disparity of understanding and misalignment across the globe—causing employees in South America to literally define one value as an unpleasant bodily function, in Australia to reject it because it was offensive, while in the United States, it had been a call to rally because of the spirit it represented. The fundamental definition of the values was not what was in question; rather, the choice of words and open interpretation they allowed. The leaders initially missed the opportunity to listen and understand across the globe how that one value could be adjusted to unite across cultures rather than to divide and be left open for interpretation.

Founder vs. Leader

We encounter many organizations in which the founder of the company remains in leadership or where his or her presence is close enough to affect decision making. The founder often brings a detailed historical perspective and a deep connection to the organization as well as a belief that they are uniquely skilled to navigate the company into the next generation. We see this in all kinds of organizations, especially in growing retail companies that began as mom-and-pop operations. In one successful retail company, in which the founder successfully navigated generations of change, the founder was unable to successfully hire his successor after years of failed attempts. He finally settled on a leader who had deep experience in the industry. Unfortunately for the business, they didn't like each other personally and could never agree on any long-term vision, only day-to-day operations. Ultimately, the only things they could agree on were watered-down give-and-takes from each of them. In short, they could agree on only the lowest common denominator solutions. This initially led to a period of acceptable returns, but over a 10-plus-year period, the sales stagnated. The impact of their misalignment was obvious to everyone but them. Only when neither of them remained in the business was the true damage revealed. Employee morale had dropped 35 percent, performance norms dropped even more dramatically, and turnover became one of the key people issues in the organization. They never understood that their dysfunction and distrust for each other had seeped out of the C-suite and permeated the entire organization.

Front of House vs. Back of House

One of the most confusing discussions I have with leaders is about front of the house versus back of the house. Talk about misalignment. What is obvious is that this creates an immediate clash between the outside and inside of a company. Yet, what is not obvious is why this even matters. After all, as people always remind us, "It is the customer who is paying the bills." Yet, time and time again, our research continues to show that in the companies that value employees and eliminate the distinction between front and back, they achieve much higher performance and increased returns.

One company created a clear literal demarcation between front of the house and back of the house. Worse than how they appointed the space was how they began to compartmentalize the space and those who occupied it, especially by where they placed the workforce who was responsible for cash flow and collecting overdue payments. Although that function was critical to operations, the perceived unpleasantness of it was hidden by placing the staff away from view. Productivity increases when staff understand the vital nature of their role, and physical cues that misalign with that importance, such as office space or lack of representation on committees, signal a misalignment. Couple that with the circuit breaker of labeling their work as something to be hidden, and you've got a potent cocktail for declining productivity that can directly affect revenue. The focus must be on the space from the perspectives of the employee and how leaders signal to them that they, the employees, are among the most important factors to the success of the business.

Values vs. Strategy

When the board of a respected, religiously affiliated health system was faced with declining business results, the leadership presented a strategy to target more affluent patients (to the exclusion of the less affluent). Their rationale was to use every marketing dollar in a highly focused way, spending only in places where the affluent target market was matched psychographically and demographically, or continue to advertise more across demographics to make all in need of their services aware. This strategy seemed reasonable, providing the increased expected revenue from more targeted advertising that would generate funds that would also support services for others in the lower socioeconomic spectrum. Theoretically, it seemed to be in alignment with their values and mission. Unfortunately for the leadership, though, the board and several of its religious board members vehemently objected to the strategy. They felt it was discriminatory, wrong, and inconsistent with the mission to serve all. This created a stalemate, leaving leadership of the health system to make a choice—do they follow the moral desires of the board and continue to spend the money in advertising and exacerbate the losses or do what they know is right for the long-term viability of their business, and ultimately, the patients they serve? The conflict between the religious, community-focused board and the business-focused leadership was real. Ultimately, the CEO was willing to risk his position based on his confidence in the strategy's ability to achieve what the system needed and what the board required. And in the end, using a highly innovative predictive model, the CEO implemented his plan, as was his prerogative. While this misalignment could not be removed or negotiated, he did create alignment for his decision by producing measurable data that gave leadership the confidence that they were making the right choice. The strategy worked and delivered financial returns of more than an 800 percent ROI. This allowed them to stay true to their mission to serve all, which was ultimately the whole goal. In the end, everyone won—especially the patients. But also, the board members who now understood that business practices could appear to be inconsistent with the mission, but in reality, was the only way to sustain it and live up to it.

People vs. Profit

Our consultants worked with a respected leader in the energy space. He was charming, honorable, and decent. We were intrigued by his soft-spoken manner and low-key commitment to his community. We were willing to do anything for this leader, because on the surface, he simply "got it." He understood what was important and how to prioritize, especially the safety of his people. Yet, over time, as we conducted site visits, we heard messages from his people that caused us to take pause. It forced us to question what was changing in his environment or in our perspective. We knew that the safety program produced significant returns—improvements of 40 percent in the first year based on decreased incidents and accidents, as well as a bonus check from the insurance company recognizing their strong safety returns. Yet, even with the successes, various elements of the effort, including employee awareness and reward programs, were excluded in the subsequent years. We thought it was strange because the ROI of the program was one of the highest we had ever seen. Then something came into focus when one of our consultants was expected to lead a leadership seminar the following afternoon. The consultant went to the airport for the quick flight the morning of the seminar. The 7 A.M. flight got canceled; then the 8 A.M. flight was canceled; then the 9 A.M. flight. It became clear that a massive storm was moving through and would not allow any flight to depart. The consultant called the client after each cancellation. The client demanded the consultant drive into the storm so he could attend the meeting. The consultant politely challenged the client about the tenets of the program and that based on all the facts, it was neither safe to fly nor drive. He offered to conduct the seminar by video. The client refused. The consultant asked me what to do, afraid that it would have a negative impact on our company if he did not put himself at physical risk and try to make it through the storm and attend. I said follow the tenets of their policy, specifically, use your best judgment. I also gave him permission to stay true to his own belief system, and ensured him that I would support him regardless of his decision. He chose to stay home—the right decision for him, his family, and our company. The misalignment revealed itself between what the client said he believed about safety and his actions, which demonstrated what he really believed about safety. Because our belief systems were so out of alignment with one another, our firm could no longer continue to work with the company.

Present vs. Future

Our charge from the CEO was simple: Help leverage the culture and drive performance across the company. For three years, we worked with the leadership to clearly define the cultural imperatives for the organization and find ways to align them across the workforce. It was working, and they were growing, with some of the largest companies in the world becoming part of their client base. As it became clear that their next evolution of growth required greater resources, they searched the globe for new financial partners. They found, after significant due diligence, ideal partners. All parties viewed the transaction favorably until the company grew rapidly. With a longer-term return strategy than the new partners were accustomed to, tension led to a misalignment, and the new partners abruptly demanded the cessation of any growth-related initiatives. The impact: no new hiring, no investment in the brand, a reduction in culture-related activities, a reduction in safety programs, and questions about the future viability of the company and of the leaders. The incongruity existed, not because the box wasn't defined, but because the leaders believed their very different worlds could co-exist and they didn't fully appreciate the nuances that were not as apparent in the other side's business. The fact remains that leaders from different industries can have the same conversations, but because they come from such different perspectives, they actually hear only the message from the priorities of their own industry, missing the intended message, and creating the misalignment that results.

Systems vs. Silos

One of the largest colleges in the country faced numerous challenges, including a diverse student population whose growth had stagnated, an intensely political board, and a brand architecture in transition. In addition to these major issues was the fact that the entire organization had an operating structure that was inefficient and designed to serve the self-interests of a select few individuals. A strong central authority was lacking with this college system and in its place was a collection of campuses that each felt like a different college. Each campus was its own fiefdom, with nothing aligned to the administration in terms of processes or curriculum. There was misalignment throughout the system, making it difficult to enact any type of system-wide initiative, ensuring change management would be hindered at every turn.

The strong, courageous leader of the system knew that a dramatic change was necessary—one that would not only remedy historical issues, but would also address their need to remain relevant for the future. The answer came in the form of a complete restructuring of the system. A number of administrative roles from each campus were brought under one central authority. The power of campus-level leadership was diminished and a solid line of authority also ran directly through the central office. The change not only ensured efficiencies of scale, but it allowed the campuses to focus on their primary mission: teaching students! A center of excellence model was also introduced that took this "hub-and-spoke" architecture to a whole new level. Instead of each campus being required to address a range of vocational training requirements and curriculum needs, a single industry-based focus was installed. Each of the campuses within the system now had an area of expertise, allowing for better utilization of resources and ensuring the best faculty were in one location with a primary focus on what they know best. The research and supporting data reinforced this strategy, showing that students who share similar interests with classmates have a higher probability of success. The synergy that came from introducing a centers-of-excellence model brought a renewed energy to the college's entire workforce and student body and brought alignment to an organization in danger of imploding.

Boards vs. Leadership

As I reflect on the relationship between boards and CEOs, I find it interesting how misalignment can become one of the key determinants of success for the CEO and the organization. More and more, the misalignment between the board and the leader simmers beneath the surface and causes great consternation for the board and a waste of time for the CEO. Increasingly, CEOs are spending time simply managing up to their boards and fulfilling requests for their bosses. Of course, this is not true for all organizations, nor is this an indictment against either the board or the leader, but it is something that does raise its head over and over. And why not? Boards are not composed of one person with one perspective; they are multiple leaders, with diverse, well-informed perspectives that can run counter to those of the CEO. While many boards understand the strict parameters of the board-CEO relationship, interested board members, often professionally talented and highly skilled, attempt to bring their expertise to support the CEO and the organization, causing further dislocation between the two functions. We are experiencing boards that struggle with understanding their role in defining a vision and the CEO's role in setting the strategy to achieve it. We are seeing boards overstep their bounds and get into the operational arena of the institution, most times to leverage their immense professional talent, although other times to undermine the CEO. Some boards create misalignment with the leader simply because they, as a board, do not agree on some issue as a board and factions need to create the misalignment to ensure that progress from the CEO is halted. We have also seen leaders reject their board's input simply because it was not that of the leader. We have seen leaders work to create wedges or withhold information (not critical information, but information that may bring color to a situation) to keep their board at a distance. We have seen instances of a number of boards and leaders who could not articulate a shared vision, creating an uncomfortable organizational dynamic that pitted a status quo against moving forward. In other cases, often in elected boards, the misalignment between members of the board and the CEO is simply political and not in the best interests of the organization they are leading. Misalignment can be the CEO simply believing his or her judgment or strategy is superior to that of the board, which often results in the eventual replacement of that leader. Regardless of the reasons, misalignment can be accidental or purposeful, but rarely does it produce the energy that moves a company forward.

Franchisee vs. Franchiser

In working with a national franchiser, we encountered misalignment throughout the company. There was the constant battle between the franchiser and franchisees, whose incentives were misaligned from the start. Complicating matters was the fact that the franchiser, a family-run operation, believed it was the right time to find an exit strategy.

Franchises often grow out of the identity of the owner, but in this case, the franchisees were operating from each of their own unique islands. There was very little agreement and less commonality from location to location. To his credit, the owner recognized that it is very difficult to sell a company that has hundreds of parts rather than one functioning whole. Every move the owner made was rebuked by the franchisees. They cared only about their immediate business results and demanded more concessions from the owner. The misalignment was palpable and could also be experienced in the stores, as each store had a different experience and the sales continued to erode, as did the value of the organization as a whole. In short, this was not working for anyone.

Many of these franchisees had invested their life savings in the franchise and considered it a cultural affront when asked to change. After all, they were chasing the American dream. But the real dream was unfulfilled, as the owner could not sell his entrepreneurial business.

The owner needed to take back control in order to create a cohesive whole that could be sold. He sought input and direction from each of his franchisees and employees. He clarified expectations for them and their customers' experience with a redefined box. He defined what it meant to be part of the company and elevated the value and perception of the brand, with redesigned stores, packaging, and promotional items. He gave where he could to support the wishes of the franchisees, and he demanded where he needed to derive value for the master brand. He gave them the perception that they were heard and increased value for their investment, even if it was in the form of a store makeover. It worked. Performance increased, the franchisees became happier and more likely to refer a friend for ownership. The franchiser was ultimately able to sell within his desired window at his desired price.

Responsibility vs. Personal Profit

A failing nonprofit healthcare system, composed of multiple primary acute-care and specialty hospitals, was still reeling from the aftershocks of a contentious merger between two religiously affiliated hospitals. Years of dysfunction had damaged these two organizations, and merging them only amplified their problems. They were two misaligned organizations that would have to quickly learn how to rely on each other and rise together or the whole system was going to be shut down and hundreds of thousands of people would be without the healthcare the system provided. They were ...

Losing money

Losing donors

Losing patients, and

On the verge of losing accreditation

One blatant piece of evidence that they were misaligned was that the doctors in this small community were the highest paid in their profession, per capita, in the country! We quickly discovered that those same doctors were partners in a large number of joint venture hospitals in which they were engaging in business practices that were beneficial to the hospitals they owned and detrimental to the health system which employed them. Although following the customs of their industry, it was certainly causing business problems by key personnel having competing priorities.

Overall, the worry-inducing and troublesome aspect of misalignment is how latent it tends to be—residing somewhere within a company's system and beyond their awareness. If there are no current crises or transitions affecting daily work and things are going "good" as usual, then it will remain dormant and quietly erode key internal functions of a company. But once a pressure point of the company gets pushed by external forces, it will emerge full-force and become a detriment to anything in its path. Unless companies commit to intentionally examining their entire system and how everything is integrated and aligned, they run the risk of missing the warning signs of misalignment.

Once misalignment is revealed, however big or small, it must be immediately addressed and acted upon. There is no quick fix to misalignment, like a Band Aid or a quick polish of a tarnished piece of silver; yet still, this is the approach many people initiate when these situations come up. Rather, issues of misalignment are like pulled muscles—they require time and precise, repetitive "stretching" in order to heal. It takes an intensive approach and an extensive process of reformation to correct the misalignment. Sometimes the misalignment is more subtle and other times it is something more overt. Regardless of the issue, it can and must be rooted out of the organization and its pysche.

The reality is that all businesses, in every state of success, experience some form of misalignment at some time in their existence. The key is to recognize the signs and to quickly get to the root of impediments and the misalignments that take the company and their people off track. Being in clarity demands not only an active view of the misalignment but a determined leader willing to do what he or she needs to break through the clutter and chaos misalignments create.

CHAPTER 4

Performance by Design

Design moves, inspires, challenges, and connects. It delights, falls flat, or disgusts. It embodies an idea and encapsulates an aspiration. It communicates quality and care. It can cheer your mood. It can touch your senses. It provides function and comfort. It interacts, charms, shelters, energizes, and calms. Design is "of our own making." It connects with us through sheer beauty or innovation. It can soften or make harder your load. Great design resonates, connects, and encourages introspective thought and meaningful action. The best design is rarely accidental in form or function.

Design is where the magic begins—inside and outside the organization. It humanizes the organization and connects the soul of the company with the heart of the employee and customer. It takes into consideration every sense, every touchpoint, and every possible experience. Design forces thought on not simply what is, rather what can be for a company and the people it touches. It encourages imagination. But, it demands discipline.

To us, every aspect of design is purposeful. And, the most impactful design is often realized when leaders understand the parameters in which they are operating, but never lose sight of the dreams they are chasing. They understand that the design is what allows connection and meaning and is what ultimately creates alignment with the clear purpose of the organization. This is the beginning of creating genuine passion by the people who drive performance on the frontlines—the employees.

That is why it is so important to not simply share, but engage and educate every person in the company on the vision so that it can be effectively and consistently seen, felt, and experienced. Design brings people, concepts, and thoughts together in a way that inspires and moves. As a social species, we are strategically designed and inclined to create a collective impact—as diverse perspectives fuel a measure of both agreement and disagreement, which universally leads to unique, highly creative solutions and innovative concepts.

Design sets the tone for attunement. We rethink and design experiences that enable people to share in a culture where they aren't merely *at* work, rather where they can become engaged in the experience *of* work. Beyond stimulating workplace culture, that engagement extends to customers and clients. It is a match that goes way beyond branding and communication to something larger: *connection*. Clarity creates the environment for connection. It makes alignment not only possible, but probable. It connects what is with what can be for every team member involved.

Performance is driven by the whole—often an inspired, aligned whole. To reach and engage an audience, the design process is central. Thus, we have always espoused the belief that design is and must be intentional. Every aspect of it. In the design of our work, there is nothing accidental—from thinking, strategy, construct, structure, content, linguistics, color, layout, and experience—to the way we want the user to consume it, interact with it, and feel about it. Design is not one-dimensional, regardless of the medium, and it is never absorbed flat. There is a dimensionality in every design and the dynamics behind how it is embraced. In the engagement of our work or the experience we create, we believe that nothing should be left to chance: All knowable factors and inputs are considered, even in a world of chaos and ambiguity. The 2014 *Forbes* piece, "Why Design Thinking

Should Be at the Core of Your Business Strategy Development," captured how design thinking creates a culture of continual improvement which can be applied to anything that needs to be improved, whether it be products, services, or processes. This intensive and intentional approach to solving problems fosters creative solutions which transcend those that are possible with more conventional modes of thinking. "This design thinking approach sets the precedent for both the consumer experience and the interactions within a company's performance." There is a reason, rationale, and definition for each element guided by the understanding that design is not about reaching some inanimate object or technology. Rather, it is about the very human relationship it establishes and the interactive space it creates.

Performance by design is about connecting where you are *now* with where you want and need to be. There's already a space where you can be better than your currently known best, and the true secret is *you already know it*. Circuit breakers, modesty, greed, and ego-serving need get in the way of you knowing you can exceed your current best. But in clarity, there is a deep comprehension of what needs to come together and connect in order to draw forth the necessary energy, ideas, and resources. Performance by design isn't something forced or hustled. It is where every intentional piece of something is designed to fit the whole. That design can be created, curated, or obtained.

You've now populated your box, understanding the six sides and all that needs to be invested in each side. You've cleared the misalignments that block and distract you, thus stealing your focus and energy. Performance by design is what elevates your workflow by engaging higher thought and deserving assurance. It brings value and worth. Design is your very personal conduit to a future state. A state in which all that you imagine and plan for, train for, and educate for, is already happening. You're just not there yet. But in clarity, you already know it exists—in possibility, capability, opportunity, promise, and vision. It just needs to be actualized. In clarity, we begin to understand everything that is needed that will serve you in that future state. Design serves as your bridge from where you are to where you want to be, and gives you a touch and glimpse of the potential to get you there.

Design for Expectation

Our team embraces opportunities when we get to work with leaders who take a more holistic view—not with a one-dimensional solution, but with a comprehensive approach anchored with great and purposeful design. The CEO of a leading industrial services company had a definitive vision for the way he wanted his company to be in the world. He wanted to be the premium player in the market, able to work with the biggest companies. Yet, he understood that in the early stages of his company's evolution, the current state, it would be challenging to compete with the industry giants toe-to-toe. He was impatient and determined, which proved to be a powerful combination as we began to innovate from the inside out. In many ways, we "manufactured" the box and put in support systems for them to be able to adopt the box that aligned with his vision. This was all about the leader and his desire to create the company in his hard-working, fiercely proud, and purposeful image. He adopted the box and literally willed the organization to follow his lead. He was clear that he wanted the design of the box to provide support systems that were embedded at every level, in order to facilitate adoption of the box and ensure that everyone had the tools to fulfill the vision.

Everything he did was purposeful. He was determined to be the leader and the change agent, and was convinced that he had not only designed a better, more high-touch service for customers, but a fundamentally redesigned experience for his craftsmen. He invested in building highly innovative and unique training centers, unlike any other competitor in their industry, and then filled them with extraordinary environmental signage and messaging to drive the values of the company. He bought into our belief that it was the expectation that defined the workplace and his company's ultimate success—but he also recognized the importance of the environment we created. He understood that his workforce had many employment options and would leave for $1 more an hour and in some cases for an increase of $.50. So, we worked with him to develop a compelling narrative that supported an almost mythological work environment whereby employees believed that there was no safer, no better, or more caring environment in which to work. He was designing an experience that no other competitor was capable of, and that his people were thirsting for. In doing so, he gave them something to rally around and believe in. He convinced them that his training was better and more focused. He convinced them that his highly personal, individualized approach to safety would get them home safe each night. He convinced them that they were part of a pack, a high-functioning team—not just a company doing work, but a tribe on a mission. Their personal stories became interwoven into the company narrative and sales materials—establishing alignment through the vehicle of purposeful participation, bestowing many with a level of respect they had never experienced.

Another part of his efforts was to incorporate trade magazines into his communication strategy. Many believed these ads were targeting potential customers; but in actuality, they were placed to speak directly to his people and build their pride. To reinforce the importance of his workforce, he created 50-foot × 50-foot permanent banners showing oversized photos of his hardest workers, with simple messages to go with each. These were then suspended on the exterior walls all around the company's main campus, so his people could see who they were through their own eyes, on a larger-than-life scale.

Every day, internally and in multiple social media outlets, they could see themselves as bigger than life—exactly as we designed. They began to believe that it was a privilege to work at the company, and not only their attitude, but their performance proved him right. His company was built to match, and even exceed, his expectations. Each dimension of the box was designed to deliver a specific aspect of what was needed to support his master design. Every physical and interactive piece of the company communicated the vision and value of the employees and their work. He envisioned a compelling future with a purposeful story, designed his box to fulfill that vision, and then built the framework for executing it. Today, they are known in the industry for a fundamentally differentiated service offering, one that has them doing business with the world's leading companies in the space. They knew they would never be the largest, but they understood the power of their differentiated box and how transformative it could be not only them, but also to their customers. And, looking back, it is clear that their success was purposeful, by design.

A WAY TO THE FUTURE

Design is both emergent and enduring. Once one bridge has served its purpose by connecting you to your desired state, you'll know more about the next design that will take you further. While people rarely talk about change in a positive light, many of us are genuinely grateful for change once it has been implemented and we are able to experience a new state. Otherwise, we'd always be content with the first thing we achieved and never have that hunger and drive for more. The energy and challenge kicked up by change serves clarity by already connecting us with the understanding that there is something better and that we're capable of more. Design helps you tap into all that your box has to offer to find solutions, inspire growth, and innovate for the future.

I frequently talk about how positivity is the glue that holds the box together. You aren't in clarity if you don't believe in the future. You aren't in clarity if you don't already know that you have more to give. Clarity helps us see how everything fits together to become whole. Clarity shows you the gaps between what exists and what needs to be developed and created. Designing for clarity translates what you see so that others can experience what you already know. We're not just creating a campaign or a slogan or an experience or a new office space. We're moving into clarity about what already exists in that desired future state and leveraging design to facilitate its emergence. Every one of your box's quadrants both benefits from and contributes to the whole. You have data that feeds understanding. You have talent that can accomplish the task. Even funding moves into the design concept when you have clarity about who your funding partner needs to be in that future state. This isn't just about the money. In clarity, you are designing for a partner that fits your plan by design, because you already know who that needs to be. Clarity allows you to recognize that essential team member by the specific contribution that only he or she can deliver. And when each piece finds its fit in your design, it is whole.

Whole Without Being Perfect

In business and in life, there is no such thing as being "perfect." Rather, there is such a thing as being "whole," which signifies the big picture as it weaves all the smaller pieces together. Being whole in this respect denotes a sense of closure that comes after all the parts fit together. Striving to be *in* clarity is about the process of becoming whole, of intentionally incorporating all the important aspects of your business into one connected form that accounts for the outside world as well. It is never, nor will it ever be, a process of perfecting and coming to completion for one moment in time. Rather, being in clarity entails a repeatable closure process, which involves adapting the whole to the surroundings in order to accommodate the changing forces exerted upon the whole. Completion or perfection describes a definitive end state, which is an irresponsible endeavor for any business, unless they plan on existing in a vacuum of time. Finding closure and sustaining the whole happens in the intermediary phase and is a reiterative activity, with an ongoing commitment to be in clarity as the moment evolves.

That being said, it is still our nature to strive for perfection as an ideal anyway. This human pursuit of ours reminds me of a story by one of my longest tenured employees. Her grandmother was a quilter. She set a goal to make a beautiful quilt for each of her many grandchildren. She carefully chose fabrics and was purposeful and intentional in choosing colors they loved and even bits of clothing that she had kept from favorite outfits they had long before outgrown. When she first started to complete the beautiful quilts, her grandchildren worried that she was becoming a little confused because they kept finding one piece in each quilt that didn't fit with the rest of the design and seemed out of place. When asked about it, she explained, "That piece is there to remind you that even though life isn't perfect, it can still be wonderful and full of love." In many ways, while different from the many client experiences we share, this story embodies what it means to be in clarity. It also suggests how *imperfections*—little quirks or flaws that exist in every facet of life, of ourselves, and of our companies—are a necessary and meaningful part of our existence. Without those slight bumps in the road or threads fraying at the end, each thing would not be our own. I've come to realize that it is the unique imperfections and idiosyncrasies which differentiate us from the rest, giving us a story that no one else has in exactly the same way.

I like to strive for a different ideal: being whole. By first accepting and then embracing that I am imperfect and always will be, it allows me to be *whole*. For designers, the best way to be successful is by creating many unique options and crafting a masterpiece out of them, which involves a lot of tinkering and iteration along the way. In fact, I've found that practicing the art of imperfection—failing fast and failing often—can lead to extraordinary results. When originating new content, any leader or designer who avoids the urge to be perfect will learn what to improve upon with each attempt they take. While they are moving forward and honing in on the right look, the person who is frozen by perfection will still be staring at a blank canvas, never breathing life into what could have been.

Symbols Unite

Let's consider the power of symbols. There is nothing more intentional than symbols in our lives and our work. These symbols help us to identify with companies, people, and groups. A critical part of branding, they give us a quick cue that we've found one of our own, something that by design fits with a part of our identity, needs, and wants. They help to form, communicate, and protect culture on the inside of the box and communicate, inspire, and make a deep connection in the environment outside our box, extending our reach to our stakeholders.

In fact, symbols and artifacts are central to our work with culture and ensure a measure of clarity as companies evolve.

Symbols elevate us to understand more and inform our thinking. Even the simplest symbol can have deep meaning. When you see a swoosh, it is not simply a mark, or swoosh. It is a well-intentioned, purposeful statement with a whole organization and defined culture behind it. When you see an associated mark, signature color, or logo, it links strategy, culture, and design. It extends the clarity that you experience and brings others into your tribe.

While I believe that creativity is a function not of time, but of talent, I have deep appreciation for the talented, highly strategic, and creative professionals who move us with their symbols and design. They drive understanding in ways the words and actions alone cannot. A strong design connects us at a visceral level, activating our senses and emotions. Think of the tied yellow ribbon hoping to bring someone home. Or, why do we all know why everything has a pink option during the month of October? Sports organizations have understood performance by design for many decades, knowing that their symbols, colors, and team spirit are inseparable, and fans fill the stadiums excited to share a common experience, which has been methodically crafted. Design transports us into a collective zone for an adventure everyone is expecting to immerse themselves in.

We use symbols as part of our work to understand, evolve, and protect culture. We utilize their power to differentiate a company and its unique position and to deliver difficult messages with ease. In an effort to drive awareness, understanding, and action around human trafficking, we developed a campaign of provocative symbols that allowed the community to put a different face or image on the daily realities of so many people trapped in unimaginable situations. The campaign used the simplicity of a symbol from an everyday street-crossing sign that is found at many intersections. However, instead of showing the universal symbol of "walk" or "don't walk," we incorporated a series of iconic and recognizable symbols to signify human trafficking. This illustrated a core design belief to us—simplicity is power. Moreover, it gave hope and a sense of understanding to people who could not read or recognize what was happening in their own lives. The symbols brought awareness to their plight and caused thousands to reach out for help.

The Virtue of Virtual

Today, as we design for performance, we have technology offering avenues for exploration beyond our imagination. More important than mere imagination, they provide us with an increasing ability to experience actual scenarios through simulations. These techniques have been used in training for many years, and recent technology has brought this ability to companies and consumers. When expensive equipment or lives are at stake, virtual simulations can mimic the experience so that training can be thorough, and the brain can become familiar with what is required. Drills are a perfect example of performance by design. Drills are based on repeated practice to instill a well-communicated set of actions and habits that are predicated by specific signals, such as an alarm going off. Through drills, we already know the behaviors that are expected. The strategy for getting out of the building has already been developed, communicated, and practiced. Once we smell smoke and hear the alarms, our adrenaline kicks into gear and our brains and central nervous system become flooded with chaos and emotion. Drills and simulations, the antidotes of uncertainty, train and prepare us to operate better under stress. They also point out misalignments and weaknesses that can be cleared or redesigned for enhanced efficiency.

We're really loving the coming attractions of gamification. It engages our spirits at a whole new level and is being used for everything from changing our eating patterns to learning better communication skills. When you gamify something, you are tapping the art of the brain that is playful and enjoys reward. The same kind of experience and participatory earning-your-place idea, such as concerts where you earn your tickets through volunteer participation, is opening the performance-by-design models to include a full range of connectivity from the simple to the sophisticated. At Deutser, gamification has become a central element in the training of our methodologies and the teaching we incorporate in our clients' learning curriculum. The technology creates a measure of alignment and ensures a consistent experience for each participant. Like all aspects of design, this becomes yet another purposeful and powerful tool not only to teach and engage, but to inspire and ensure clarity, employee by employee.

Design Delivery

While every form of design is important and informs in different and unique ways, so, too, must the delivery mechanism of a highly designed piece, event, experience, training, or package be equally well thought out. This was especially true for our team when we had the opportunity to introduce a fundamentally rethought, high-end grocery store concept to its employees. The stores were spectacular. And so, too, was the expectation for the employees to live up to the very explicit values and behaviors the company defined. In their stated culture, the employees were considered the hosts and the customers were to be treated as the guests. This was about creating a highly differentiated shopping experience, so when it came time to educate and acculturate the employees, it demanded something as creative and fresh as the store experience itself.

We designed an experience and learning program called Street Smart. The theme was about ingraining the culture and making the expected behavior as natural as possible, giving the tools and training for each employee to become not only knowledgeable, but street-smart.

We invited employees to the training with elaborate invitations to whet their appetites. When they entered the training session, the experience began by engulfing them in the new identity emblazoned everywhere in the room. The room was designed in the shape of their round logo, which had a giant spoon image at the heart of it, which was translated into a unique spoon-shaped runway.

People were excited, but confused as we began to introduce them to the new concept. Each was given a nametag, not with their name, but with similar items—that is, one had fish sticks, the other had sushi—and they had to socialize and figure out which team they would be part of for the training. Every element was carefully designed to educate, inform, excite, and connect the employees. Following the introduction, the logo was brought out on individual cakes, expertly crafted by their bakers, to demonstrate the new level of taste they would bring to their food and service. The leadership then stepped foot on the spoon-shaped runway, donning the new uniforms to hoots and hollers from the employees. Throughout the day, employees were awarded with puzzle pieces based on their learnings and understanding of the values and behaviors to create and finish their own puzzle (in the shape of the new logo).

We are always learning and teaching as leaders. The key is to recognize that sometimes being purposeful and thoughtful with how the information is delivered can be more impactful and transformative than the basic message itself, especially when we are trying to change people's minds. On the surface this seems like outside-the-box thinking. But in reality, every creative concept came from inside the box—the box informed and drove creativity from inside in a brand-centric manner. We leveraged every part of the box as we dreamed up this experience, balancing direction and operations with the people and engagement perspectives. This gave us a measure of connection with the employees to ensure a rare experience that they would never forget. The idea was if it was memorable enough and if they felt special enough, then they could advance that same feeling to their guests.

ELEGANCE VERSUS EGO

There is a wonderful, elegant dance to the solution that takes place in the "coming together" of something—the one-of-a-kind way that completes. The way the outcome or appearance of it becomes evident. We see it in mathematic equations, complementary colors, and musical phrases. There's a balance and beauty in the answer. It is as if we've uncovered something that was already meant to fulfill the vision rather than conjuring it up ourselves.

As individuals and leaders, it can be exhilarating to encounter those moments of discovery. A colleague recently took her kids to a museum where there were play stations of puzzles and riddles to solve. One had four capital T's that you had to lay flat within a large and then a small square frame. They fit perfectly within the large square. But then, when they tried the small square, they just didn't fit. They nestled and turned them every which way they could, but the fourth T just would not fit inside the frame. It seemed impossible. Finally, when they turned them on the diagonal, they fit! It was elegant and beautiful the way they fit together, like a turning wheel. Then it looked easy, like it was meant to be.

Good design is like that. We fumble around and try things until the perfect solution appears. There's an order and a flow to the universe that we can't see, but we can feel. We recognize when it's right. The funny thing is, up until the moment you find the solution, you feel as though it's impossible to solve. But, in clarity, we learn how to look in the right direction. We can see to try it on the diagonal!

Maximizing Space

There is great power with a well-designed trade show exhibit or display. While the space at a conference varies and there are a host of booth sizes to navigate, many companies invest in smaller, more traditional-sized booths with just enough space for signs and people to gather. While we encourage purposefulness of design with these smaller booths to maximize space, we also go to great lengths to find interesting ways to use design to deliver a message and connect people.

One unique and challenging space we created was at a large trade show that showed off technology as well as impressively large machines and transport vehicles in the healthcare sphere. The challenge was that it was one of our client's first trade shows and we had a small, misshaped 20-foot × 10-foot island compared to our competitor's space: a high-profile-50-foot × 50-foot booth in a prime location. Regardless of the circumstances, our client demanded that we make an impression. Our feeling was, "Let's go for it!" This sounds like an outside-the-box moment, but again the smaller space dictated a measure of attention that required creative solutions from within. And, our box was defined literally by the space we were assigned.

While our client's technology was superior to their competitors, we didn't have the ability to show it off because of space and budgetary constraints. So, we differentiated them by showcasing safety in a unique and somewhat risky way. We convinced the client that we should wrap one of their ambulances in bubble wrap, every square inch of it, from top to bottom and then put a small sign on the bubble wrap that read: "Some people think we are a little obsessed with safety. We are." We added under the message in small type: winner of the industry safety award. It was an intentional, but scary thought to attempt something so different at the largest and only trade show for their industry. In fact, the client said, "If this doesn't work, this will be your first and last show with us." We loved the challenge of conjuring up the concept and then executing it. Nearly a decade later, the bubble wrap is still the talk of the show, and our work continues with the client, proving that it is not the constraints of which we have little control; rather, it is the creativity inspired from within that will define our outcome.

LINGER IN THE QUESTION (AND LISTEN)

The longer we stay in the question and ruminate there, the more obvious the answer will be. There are times that we jump to conclusions or answers that worked for other problems. Instead, empathetically put yourself in the shoes of the person you're trying to make a connection with, not just to get their attention, but to truly connect. What do they care about? What motivates them? What's their situation? What are they dealing with every day? Then, ask a new set of questions: What specifically do we want them to think, feel, or do differently in the future? Working backward from those questions often illuminates several possible solutions.

One example is the concept of utilitarian design. Ever notice how when finding one's way in a new city, we can get very frustrated by poor signage? Clearly, whoever was designing it didn't take the time to drive or walk the path. On the other hand, good signage usually goes unnoticed because it is clear and does its job. It just feels like it belongs in the space—it works without trying or being forced. Does it drive anyone else crazy that in many public restrooms, the stall door opens inward, so you have to back up and sometimes touch the toilet to get out? Or that the paper towel dispenser is often placed too high, so water runs down your arm while you're trying to dry your hands? Being thoughtful and empathetic about the experience people will have can make a huge difference.

Be Cause

Throughout my career, I have had the privilege to work for a wide assortment of leaders. Many were visionary, creative, and purposeful in all their actions. Others were less engaged, more reckless, and self-centered. In their own way, each taught me the value and importance of leadership. They also showed me how leadership can inspire, tear down, baffle, and build up.

For nearly a decade, I was mesmerized by one of the leaders who rarely shared information, only giving people closest to him just enough details to be satisfied. He had an uncanny ability to keep the company profitable without ever really moving it forward. It was here that I learned that companies are often created to serve someone's best self-interest. In this case, it was his interest that was being served. And, while the focus of the most purposeful leaders is to grow while navigating the chaos in the world, his efforts were to ensure status quo. Why? Because the status quo ensured his way of life and his control of the business. He knew that if he grew the business, it would require new leadership to support the growth, which he believed could result in losing control. In the end, he maintained his business at its level until he died—unfortunately, leaving very little, including a legacy.

This is in contrast to another leader for whom I worked whose purpose was far different. This leader was determined to leave a positive legacy for herself and every client she touched. She designed a company that on the outside was clearly intended for women and their advancement. (I was there as an early "token male" due to the needs of a demanding client who wanted at least one male at the table. This experience evolved into being perhaps the most growth-orienting and mind-altering opportunity of my life—demonstrating what it felt like to be the outsider.) But in reality, this was not just about a place for women. This leader had a laser-like focus on one area and one area only—being socially responsible and changing the world by connecting companies with causes and doing good for others. She was fully focused on growing and making a mark, understanding that being intentional about her purpose was the key to her growth and sustainability. She turned business away that did not align with the firm's or her vision and values. She was unafraid to take chances and fail—knowing that her endgame was creating something much larger than ever existed in the space. She was determined to stand for something unique and made sure her clients did as well. Her expectations, which I often believed were unreasonable, inspired a bigger way of thinking and level of creativity that was unique.

She inspired us to create socially responsible programs, inside each client's unique box, that redefined industry and changed lives. We created never-before seen events in the center of the concourse at Grand Central Station for an international client—using 60-foot half pipes as the backdrop for an innovative demonstration for the media. We never imagined it would bring the rush-hour pedestrian traffic inside to a halt as well, but it did. We sent things through the U.S. Postal Service that were shocking, including jars of water with leather gloves (to prove the point that our leather dried faster and softer than any other leather), chattering teeth, hot-pink-spray-painted shock absorbers, redesigned ketchup bottles, and so much more. Each were sent for impact. In fact, everything she did was designed for impact—human impact. She was far ahead of her time and has created a movement in the cause marketing space because she believed in her purpose. Ultimately, she sold her firm; but more than just that, she sold her vision of how companies can help communities all over the world. Now they, too, believe in the power of purpose.

Design Your Mindset

While many leaders focus on what is next and how to create the biggest impact, we often overlook the here and now and the power of the moment in which we are living and working. We have found, through our studies on understanding the science of the brain as it relates to safety and overall performance, especially in environments which demand accuracy for employees conducting repetitive tasks, that we have far more control over our brains than we think.

Therefore, we have designed programs for clients to help educate employees around the power that each and every person has in directing their thinking and designing their desired outcomes. We have taken this even further with spaces and exercises to improve the efficiency and effectiveness of meetings. In our company, we have begun to norm some of our meeting behaviors using space to direct the mind. With our theme-driven collaboration stations throughout the office (explained in greater detail in Chapter 5), we have encouraged specific types of conversations to take place at certain places: colorful and creative conversations in one place, sticky conversations in one place, and grounded conversations in one place. It does not preclude people from meeting in other places, it simply conditions the mind to almost immediately be in the moment with a defined mindset for that type of conversation.

We have also recognized that leaders and employees are constantly navigating between not only work challenges, but home and life challenges as well. We are inundated with deadlines, meetings, email, texts, calls, and other interferences which can take us out of any given moment. Yet, we are expected to "be on" and ready to perform in every meeting. In our company, we can go from meetings on a highly strategic corporate issue to impacting a crisis situation to developing a creative engagement campaign in the span of a morning. We recognized that it was taking our team too long to get in the moment of the next meeting and to switch gears and change their perspectives as they navigated between vastly different topics that required different mental states. That is why we decided to create a series of exercises using color, which we call Huemanize Mind Maps (See Figure 2.1), to norm the mind of the individual and group as we shift from one meeting to another. By using color, we have been able to get into meetings much quicker and with more effective and appropriate outcomes and far less wasted time.

We have long believed that when you change your mindset, you can change your outcomes. The mind does what we condition and tell it to do. We are in control of what we think and where we allow our minds to take us. Ingraining the discipline of mindfulness and ensuring purposeful thinking, by leaders and employees, will elevate productivity and performance. Again and again, we go back to the concept of environment versus expectation—when we set the expectation of ourselves and the people around us, we are in effect helping them to create a more purposeful pathway and to design their future.

HUEMANIZE MIND MAPS

Before going to any meeting or tackling any task, you can reframe your mindset with the aid of this color-themed exercise. (Step 1) Identify a color from below that reflects your desired mindset or outcome. (Step 2) Reflect on the corresponding exercises from the following pages to reframe your perspective. (Step 3) Repeat throughout your day as needed.

big thinking, no limits	complete serenity	fun, get-it-done attitude	navigating challenges
can do nothing wrong	holistic approach	growth mentality	absolute clarity
coast + chill	say what you think	mysterious, miraculous mindset	we're all in this together
enthusiastic + confident	i need a cup of coffee first	help me out, i'm stuck	energy all over the place

Figure 4.1   Huemanize Mind Maps

BLUE SKY (BIG THINKING, NO LIMITS)

An open, imaginative mindset characterized by higher-level thinking and a forward-driven approach; looking beyond the current details to imagine what's possible in the future.

SETTING THE ENVIRONMENT

Imagine you are in a vast open area looking out at a clear, blue sky. As you enjoy the depth of the sky, you begin to notice all the different hues of blue above you.

EXERCISES

1. If you could be anywhere in the world, doing anything you want with no limits, where would you be?

2. Create the transportation vehicle of the future. It is up to you what it looks like, how it operates, and where it can take you. Start imagining!

3. Picture having a crystal ball in front of you—you can envision the future of anything with it. What is the world you hope to see 10 years from now?

BEACHY BEIGE (COMPLETE SERENITY)

A relaxed, undistracted mindset focused on the present; feeling composed in the situation, reserved in energy, and openly receptive with whatever unfolds before you.

SETTING THE ENVIRONMENT

Imagine sitting in the sand on a private beach, with no one else around and the sun setting in the distance.

EXERCISES

1. Think of a place that made you feel tranquil and relieved. What did it look like and more importantly, how did it make you feel?

2. Imagine your favorite outlook spot possible. What type of nature is before your eyes, and what sounds do you hear around you?

3. Meditate for 5 minutes—focusing solely on the image of yourself on the beach. If your mind wanders, then gently redirect your thinking back to the warm breeze on your beach chair.

POSITIVELY PINK (FUN, GET-IT-DONE ATTITUDE)

An easy-going, lighthearted attitude where everyone is free to creatively express themselves and explore the task at hand; feeling positive and high in energy, where one is encouraging of self and others.

SETTING THE ENVIRONMENT

Imagine being in a vibrant, bright pink room with all the walls highlighted with large polka dots and bold stripes and filled with beanbag chairs and fun accessories. Everything about the environment is light and fun.

EXERCISES

1. Think about a song that is the most fun for you to listen to. Play it or sing it in your mind with the real words or your made-up words.

2. Take your name and design a personal logo, tagline, motto—explore whatever comes to mind.

3. Doodle something fun for 45 seconds.

DARK CLOUD (NAVIGATING CHALLENGES)

A serious, methodical approach toward challenges that best positions oneself to see the obstacles ahead as opportunities; thinking that is objective and realistic about the hardships ahead, which allows one to move forward with mindfulness and precision.

SETTING THE ENVIRONMENT

Imagine yourself driving on a highway, heading directly into a thunderstorm that is heavy, gray, and inevitable to avoid. Recognize the extreme focus, patience, and caution you will have to take to safely navigate.

EXERCISES

1. Think of a challenging experience you've worked to overcome. How did you approach it? What did you learn in the process?

2. Imagine you are a ship captain on rough seas. From a leadership standpoint, how do you communicate with the crew to prepare them for the incoming challenge?

3. Identify a time in your life when you were in a serious situation (real or imagined), and your decisions determined your outcome?

ORANGE U HAPPY (CAN DO NOTHING WRONG)

A stimulated, go-getter mentality where there is an unflinching belief that whatever you say, believe, or do will turn out great; a magical state that encourages idea sharing and unfiltered creativity, which unleashes a positive energy that is contagious.

SETTING THE ENVIRONMENT

Imagine being in a bright, orange room filled with streams of light from the sun and decorated with giant smiley faces, your favorite motivational quotes, and your favorite music blaring in the background.

EXERCISES

1. Remember a time when everything you did worked. Recapture the magical feeling when everything was easy, light, and turned to gold.

2. Free-write about something you love, or a time you had great success.

3. What is an all-time favorite hobby of yours? Describe how you feel when you're doing it and achieving your very best outcomes.

PURE WHITE (HOLISTIC APPROACH)

A pure, "everything is connected, no judgment" state of mind, looking at the whole picture to see all the interactions between the parts; an open-minded, all-encompassing method of perceiving something, to capture the essence of every part involved.

SETTING THE ENVIRONMENT

Imagine being in a room with white floors, white walls, white ceilings, white conference table and chairs and white-backed glass panels to encourage creative expression and no outside influence. The only color in the room is that of the mind and the magic markers to fill the glass boards where you can see out over the entire city.

EXERCISES

1. Stare at a white sheet of paper and begin to draw simple pictures with a white pen in your mind.

2. Close your eyes, and focus on your breathing. Slowly breathe in, hold the air, and slowly release it. As you feel the breath going through your body, imagine a white cleansing light beginning to permeate your body. The white light brings clarity of thought and emotion.

3. Imagine floating in a cloud where you can see all that is going on down below. What does the city look like from up here? What patterns do you see that you wouldn't normally see on the ground?

GREEN FIELD (GROWTH MENTALITY)

Grow, grow, grow is the mantra — everything you think, do and say is about moving forward and expanding thought, boundaries, and horizons; a flexible, practice-oriented approach to growth and improvement; an optimistic thinking style that expresses the plasticity of an individual and the potential one is capable of actualizing.

SETTING THE ENVIRONMENT

Imagine being in nature in an empty, open green field. As you stand in the center of the field, large trees begin to sprout and grow all around you, and flowers begin to pop out and bloom.

EXERCISES

1. Think about a time you built or created something from scratch with or without directions. What was it? How did you feel after completing it?

2. Recall a time you set a personal or professional goal and met it. What steps did you take to get there?

3. Think about your body and physical health. What is one thing that is strong, and why is it that way, or how do you manage to keep that strength there? What is something that you could work on and get better at? What is the future self you see if, or when, you strengthen those muscles or parts of your body?

DEUTSER RED (ABSOLUTE CLARITY)

An eager leadership mindset and visionary approach, filled with contagious inspiration, inner courage, and outward-facing charisma; a feeling of intuition, excitement, and energy that highlights possibilities and evokes hope in others.

SETTING THE ENVIRONMENT

Imagine standing in a vibrant red room, the walls are high gloss with lights from the ceiling adding additional sheen. In the center of the back wall rests a bullseye with Deutser Red at the center.

EXERCISES

1. You are the president of the United States for a day. What is the first message you will deliver to the country?

2. Recall a time where you lead a group to success, even when it didn't seem possible. How did you inspire others to get on board and ultimately win?

3. Think about your body/physical health. What is one thing that is strong, and why is it that way, or how do you manage to keep that strength there? What is something that you could work on and get better at? What is the future self you see if, or when, you strengthen those muscles or parts of your body?

EASY-BREEZY YELLOW (COAST + CHILL)

A laid-back, calm and collected mindset that allows one to reserve their energy and see things from a broader perspective; feeling peaceful and concentrated on the moment; viewing life from the "passenger's seat," relieved from panic or preoccupation.

SETTING THE ENVIRONMENT

Imagine being on a drive down the coast in a convertible with the sun rising softly in the distance and a gentle breeze filling the car, as the yellow rays play off the cliffs near the road and shine through the clouds.

EXERCISES

1. Remember a time when someone helped navigate you through an assignment, and all you had to do was go along for the ride.

2. Just shut your eyes and breathe deep, inhaling for 6 seconds, followed by an exhale for 6 seconds. Just imagine the calm going over and through your whole body—only focusing on the breath and the peace around you.

3. Imagine arriving in your favorite city, with nothing on your agenda. As part of your trip, you are granted a chauffeur to take you anywhere you want to go. Where would you go? What sights would you see? How would it feel sitting in the passenger's seat, simply taking it all in?

ESPRESSO YOURSELF (SAY WHAT YOU THINK)

An inspired and deeply convicted attitude toward sharing one's insight or perspective on topics that are personally and professionally relevant; a mentality characterized by sharpened cognition and high energy, where one is openly expressive of ideas and speaks up and out without hesitation.

SETTING THE ENVIRONMENT

Imagine sitting in oversized, soft leather chairs with your best friend in a coffeehouse, with a fresh cup of coffee in your hand and feeling the safety in knowing that no topic is off limits.

EXERCISES

1. Rapid-fire association exercise: With the words listed below, think about the first few words or ideas that come to mind in the line(s) provided.

    Social Justice _____

    Government/Politics _____

    Religion/Spirituality _____

    Favorite Team _____

    Favorite Cause _____

    Love _____

    Playtime _____

2. Remember the most outspoken thing you have ever done or thought about in your life? How did it make you feel? How did others react to you?

3. Deliver an extemporaneous, 60-second stump speech for the political candidate of your choosing.

BLUE MIST (MYSTERIOUS, MIRACULOUS MINDSET)

A brooding intellectual state, where one is deep in thinking, slower to act and struggling to arrive at an answer but confident that a solution will mysteriously appear; feeling bogged down by worry, angst, or indecision about a certain situation or task.

SETTING THE ENVIRONMENT

Imagine sitting alone on a dark, moonlit night outside on a park bench as a light mist gently awakens the senses.

EXERCISES

1. Remember a time when you desperately needed an answer to a question and it miraculously came to you.

2. Think about a movie where you expected an outcome, but the actual outcome surprised you and was far better than you imagined.

3. Identify three things that you consider to be among the greatest mysteries in the world.

    1. _____

    2. _____

    3. _____

OLIVE U (WE'RE ALL IN THIS TOGETHER)

An inclusive, team-based approach which incorporates others and appreciates their thoughts and contributions; focusing on the collective ability of a group and the shared energy toward an overall goal; taking a complimentary, comprehensive viewpoint of the team.

SETTING THE ENVIRONMENT

Imagine sitting around minutes before the big game in an old fashioned locker room with your teammates. There are confident stares all around with members of the team periodically making eye contact with teammates seated across from them.

EXERCISES

1. Reflect back to the best team or group you've been a part of. Who were the "key leaders," and how did each person contribute to the overall functioning and success of the team?

2. Think about your favorite sports team or arts group. How do they make all the varying parts fit together and create a winning combination? In your organization or your family unit, how do the strengths and weaknesses fit together?

3. Remember a time when the individual solution you created was not nearly as powerful as your team/department's collective solution.

JUST PEACHY (ENTHUSIASTIC + CONFIDENT)

An enthusiastic mindset characterized by positive thinking and a group-oriented approach; feeling inspired, high in energy and spirited, and willingly transmitting that to others.

SETTING THE ENVIRONMENT

Imagine standing in a room washed by warm, welcoming peach lighting and encircled by a group of people who admire and look up to you.

EXERCISES

1. If you were asked to give a TED talk, what is a fun, upbeat story you'd share with the audience?

2. What is the one thing about you that inspires you and makes you feel most proud?

3. Give an imaginary pep talk to a group of 7-year-olds as they are about to take the field for a big game.

PURPLE DAZE (I NEED A CUP OF COFFEE FIRST)

A low-energy, lethargic, overly relaxed mentality; feeling disinterested in interactions or disengaged in the present moment; an apathetic, avoidant style of approaching complex issues.

SETTING THE ENVIRONMENT

Imagine sitting in a dimly lit room, surrounded by a thick purple fog that is hard to see through.

EXERCISES

1. Remember a story that your parents told you or read to you as a child to get you relaxed before bedtime.

2. Stand up and take some time to stretch, activating every muscle in your body.

3. Get up and go pour yourself a cup of coffee or a big glass of cold water.

BLACK HOLE (HELP ME OUT, I'M STUCK)

A heavy mindset which feels overwhelmed and immobile; feeling firmly fixed in a problem, challenged to see new possibilities beyond one's current viewpoint; fixating on shortcomings and what's been done wrong instead of highlighting what's right or what's possible.

SETTING THE ENVIRONMENT

Imagine being at the bottom of a deep hole outside at night and needing the help of others to comfort you and eventually pull you out.

EXERCISES

1. Visualize being caught in quicksand (which represents your current thoughts and feelings surrounding a topic). Now, think about the three people you can call for help to pull you out of your funk.

2. You are lost in a foreign city on a walk through a dark neighborhood with only a dimly lit flashlight. How do you navigate your way out of the situation to safety?

3. Think about calling someone who has helped you out of a difficult situation before, and thank them for their help.

SPLATTER/TIE-DYE (ALL OVER THE PLACE)

An explosive, explorative mentality that freely moves from one perspective to another; a quick-shifting mindset that creatively expresses multiple takes on one idea or topic.

SETTING THE ENVIRONMENT

Imagine being a kid again and playing in a multicolored ball pit. Visualize the freedom of throwing the balls at the nets, jumping around, swimming amongst the balls, and doing whatever you want in the color-filled ball pit.

EXERCISES

1. Free-write for one minute about anything and everything on your mind—with the goal of putting as many thoughts down as possible (and rarely finishing any thought).

2. Identify 10 fun, wild, out-there things that only you could ever dream about bringing to a family picnic.

3. Think about your five favorite songs. In your mind, sing your favorite verse of each, rapidly shifting from one to the other.

POSITIVITY

The power of the mind for convincing people that they can achieve at higher levels than they ever imagined is core to our success. We have worked with leaders and organizations that believed they could achieve greatness, and in virtually every case, they did. We have worked with companies that believed they could be good, and that is as high as they wanted to be. Defining the expectation and then living up to it is at the heart of purposeful design. For more than two decades, I have worked with a high-end retail company. They have been successful by remaining true to their core product. They experienced double-digit growth year after year by focusing on what they did best. Then the market changed. Imports (not American-made) became the industry norm. The economy turned and a slew of competitors entered the market. Their core product no longer enjoyed the same success they had previously experienced. They literally watched their industry change around them—secondary products, with much greater margin than their core products, were afterthoughts to them. Their competitors leveraged the secondary products much more quickly and drove profitability. This high-margin product, which accounted for 9 percent of our client's business, was becoming nearly 30 percent of their competitors' business. Yet, our client purposely stayed away from growing that segment, believing it was inconsistent with their image. Then, a leadership change occurred, accompanied by a mandate of immediate growth and increased returns to their parent company. The area for immediate impact was obvious—this underperforming segment. Before changing the display or bringing in extra product, the new CEO designed his effort around his team that sold the product. He convinced the organization that this segment was important. He positively included it in every message, in every report, and in every personal interaction with salespeople. He upped the incentive and made sure that it was the same for everything they sold, regardless of what was sold. But more than anything, he convinced the entire workforce that this was important and that they could be successful. He was right. After three months, performance in that area alone increased by more than 180 percent, proving that if you design to believe, you can achieve. By altering the expectations in the workforce and incentivizing them to buy into and believe in the new approach, the rest will follow as their actions realign.

Leaving Baggage Behind

While we place great emphasis and attention on intentionality and the expectations we set, the overall environment matters as well. When we were building out our new offices, we understood that the design of the new space would be transformative in how we worked, in how we interacted, and how we perceived our work. We also realized that while the space was critical to all we were doing, what mattered most was the intentionality of the moment before we moved. In other words, we had to mentally prepare to go to a different, much more creative work environment.

Our challenge was to bring with us only what mattered most and what we needed to bring. This is an impossible task for a person like me who loves paper. But this was not about packing papers and old artifacts that defined our culture. This was about bringing with us only the behaviors and attitudes that would be consistent to where we were going. So we put a large suitcase at the entrance of our old space. It was there for a week, open and empty, for every employee to pass by. Finally, I shared the intentionality of the suitcase—telling everyone that they would be required to leave any and all old baggage behind. The old tapes of how we did things or who said what to whom had to be "packed away." The disagreements were left behind. It was about setting up the positivity our new environment required and allowing a purposeful connection to the space long before we moved in. Obviously, the suitcase was a metaphor; but in many ways, it was the most intentional and important part of our move.

Every day, leaders have a choice to make. How will they design their day? Or, will they allow it to be defined for them?

Morning Clarity

Every great leader brings a personal discipline and clear set of habits to each day. I focus a great deal on being purposeful and positive with my actions and words. I start each day with several exercises to ensure a measure of focus and purpose. I find that when I do not have a plan, my day often becomes either someone else's or a day of reaction, thereby limiting my effectiveness and masking the clarity needed to perform at my highest level.

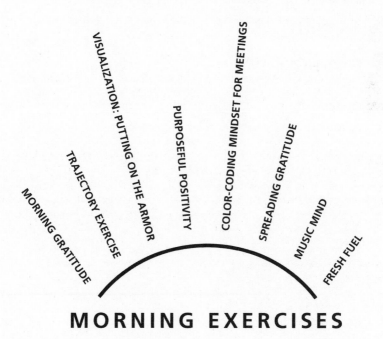

Figure 4.2   Morning Clarity

🧍 MORNING GRATITUDE

After waking up, I gather my thoughts and extend my arms upward, expressing gratitude for all I've received, and all I am hoping to achieve. It is all about starting with reflection and a moment of self-awareness to start the day.

Activity: Express gratitude in your mind for all you've experienced and achieved.

📍 TRAJECTORY EXERCISE

I've identified a drawing (a mandala that's appropriately titled Trajectory) that helps me define my purpose and direction for the day. I take time to gaze at it, which brings things to my awareness that I wasn't focused on before. Then, I set a purposeful intention on what I will achieve that day, and write it down on a card that I keep in my pocket all day.

Activity: On a piece of paper, set one positive trajectory you'll achieve today and keep it in your pocket.

🏃 VISUALIZATION EXERCISE: LAYER OF PROTECTIVE ENERGY

Each morning before I get out of bed or check my phone, I go through a mental exercise where I imagine wrapping my body in protective energy or armor. This imagined layer reinforces the idea that only I can allow negativity or outside influences to enter my space and take me off-target.

Activity: Before you get out of bed, visualize wrapping yourself in some protective coating. Think about what is under your control—your intentions, your energy, your reactions, and your effort.

📋 PURPOSEFUL POSITIVITY

Before I leave the house, I write down one thing I will leave behind from the day before, one thing I will carry forward from the day before, and one new thing I will seek out in my day.

Activity: Before you leave the house, write down three positive affirmations about your abilities, your achievements, or your dreams for the future on a piece of paper.

🌈 COLOR-CODING MINDSET FOR MEETINGS

Before beginning my workday, I will look at my agenda and "color code" each of the meetings with the mentality it requires, using the proprietary system we have. For example, a challenging, contentious meeting will require a "dark cloud" mindset (gray), versus a creative meeting, which requires a "fun, get it done attitude" (pink).

Activity: Take your daily agenda, and jot down a few words about the attitude or mentality it will require. Then, using the Huemanize color sheet (see appendix), color-code each of those attitudes.

SPREADING GRATITUDE

I spend a few minutes sending a message to someone else, thanking them and appreciating who they are. This small message energizes me and often results in a positive response back, becoming a win-win situation. And, I identify my release valve for the day—someone to whom I can release negative energy, or someone from whom I get positive reinforcement.

Activity: Send a message to someone you're thankful for—it can be hand-written or digital. Be specific and make it personal.

MUSIC MIND

I try to create my daily playlist. Although this is not a real playlist, it is virtual; this forces me to concentrate on the songs in my head. Thus, it forces what I am listening to in a purposeful way instead of just listening to the news or talk radio.

Activity: Before heading out the door, make a mental list of three songs that are important or inspiring to you. Then, as you begin your day, verbalize them in your mind and engage the emotions they bring.

FRESH FUEL

Before eating breakfast, I will find something fresh and sweet to put into my body, signifying both a fresh beginning for today and a purposeful release of yesterday.

Activity: Before eating breakfast, eat two pieces of your favorite fruit or sweet. As you eat the first one, reflect on the energy you will bring today. As you eat the second one, reflect on the negative energy from yesterday that you will leave behind.

I have always believed that purposeful and intentional design extends to how a leader's day is framed and actualized. It is why I have ascribed a daily routine to ensure I have the proper mindset as I venture forward. To me, the morning clarity exercise helps to prepare, protect, and challenge me to achieve all that is ahead.

DESIGN IS FOUNDATIONAL

Design is the medium that helps to define the soul of an organization, directing the interactions that take place there, the way people perform, and the impression that gets left behind. Whether you are creating a customer experience, building and outfitting an office space, or creating the iconic symbol that you will become known by, the design process is inextricably linked to everything that your company will be. Design is the essential component that sustains and elevates the function and performance of your company from both the macroscopic and microscopic level. It creates a tangible, visible persona, with an invisible energy that affects anyone that interacts with your company. It brings forward your deepest identity, expressing a story that words alone could not master. For a customer or end user, design acts as a window into the mind and heart of your company, like an access point with universal appeal that transcends the language barrier. Design creates an undeniable connection that moves us collectively, operating as a totem that can guide and inspire for those both inside and out.

CHAPTER 5

Impact Drivers

D eutser has been built on the firm belief that finding and leveraging the positive side, even in the most serious and grave environments, is what separates great companies and leaders from merely good ones. When we understand at a fundamental level, and deeply embrace what is central, enduring, and distinct about our organization, others will join in work with shared passion to encourage and ultimately achieve alignment. What makes a positive culture? Leaders in touch with their people and people aligned with the organizational expectations.

Most organizations overlook the impact of culture. One of our objectives is always to help leaders understand their culture for what it is and to be able to identify what they want and need it to be. We work to bridge the gap between the current and future state. In our work, we have taken a different tack from most consultants, who primarily focus on identifying problems and correcting them. In our process, leaders emphasize positivity and focus on what is and what is possible in equally positive ways. That is why we start with the box. When we return to our *shared* identity, characteristics, values, and traditions, it helps us to genuinely connect through what is shared and similar rather than to disconnect through what is different and troublesome. Some might scoff at positive psychology and the power of positive thinking, but I have seen how authentic positivity holds an organization's box together and gives it a vibrancy that strengthens and enriches an organization's culture.

Organizations that find ways to infuse a positive outlook with an authentic sense of optimism at their core experience measurably improved performance and motivation among employees. Fundamental to our approach to positivity is our belief that the vast majority of companies are built on good, pure, and positive intentions. That same measure of positivity that once existed at the beginning of our company still exists today and it's the leader's imperative to be constantly searching for those origins of innate positivity. This foundation is at the heart of what we do at Deutser to help organizations truly transform.

But it is incumbent upon the leader to truly understand the people who are driving not simply the performance but the overall culture and attitudes of the company. While the leader is the *ultimate* definer and driver of culture, we must recognize that there are personalities within our organizations that intentionally or unintentionally move us closer to or farther away from the desired culture. We employ exercises to help leaders identify these defining personalities within their own company (See Figure 5.1).

Our work is helping leaders address the ambiguity in the workplace, navigating challenges, "winning" their transitions, and achieving a level of performance. It all requires a seriousness of thought and measure of belief, the optimistic quotient again, that your future can be an even better version of your past and that you have some measure of control on what it will look like. In other words, there are no accidents when it comes to your desired future performance state. It is purposeful, well defined, and actionable. Most leaders embrace this ideology—or they wouldn't be leaders. They have confidence and experience to know that their inputs matter and define the ultimate outputs and results of the company. Again, it goes back to purpose and intentionality. It is not doing something just to do it, but doing something on purpose with the endgame in mind.

Through our work and research, we've identified 11 levers that together will shift the organization toward positivity and drive performance. We work with leaders to identify the best ways to pull these levers to make an impact inside their unique organizations. Hay Group explains the importance of focusing on the right culture levers. They state, "Another mistake that many organizations make is trying to change too many things at once, often focusing on communications, training, and internal marketing campaigns which can be overwhelming, superficial, and short-lived. It is also important to identify the positive elements of the current culture that should be kept and reinforced in the future. It is unlikely that an organization needs to undertake a complete change of all the attributes of its culture. Therefore, the transformation should focus just on the elements that need to change or be realigned."

These 11 levers have power and bring results. As we studied what truly brought about positive change in organizations, we saw that it wasn't only the lever itself, it was the calibration in the deployment of the lever. There is a level of work that looks pretty good, but is merely an effort that is being compliant. In other words, they are "fine." Things go along and don't cause problems. They bring results that are "good enough." They check the boxes of requirement and they mostly keep things humming along with occasional high fives. But good is the enemy of great and if you want a lever to bring change, you have to move from being compliant with efforts that look or seem like the effort is there, to committed, where your very being is invested in both the endeavor and the expectation of impact. Although to the rest of the world, compliant looks like you are accomplishing something, we identify it for what it is—checking boxes and underperforming—whereas, with commitment, we appropriately recognize it for creating impact.

THE SITCOM

You are creating a television sitcom based on the people you work with in your office (or people closest to you in your life). The purpose of this exercise is to recognize the different personalities and people characteristics that both create your workplace and define your culture. Think about the whole of your environment before you start describing each of the "starring characters" of your sitcom.

1. Based on your environment, what is the most compelling show name or title that would describe your workplace and the show you are creating?

2. Identify four "personalities" in your work or personal environment that represent the high performer, the big personality, the low performer, and the office leader.

3. Name your characters (real or fictional name). Do they need a nickname (i.e. people pleaser, showman, wonder woman, the judge, naysayer, the gossip, etc)?

4. Draw a stick figure or fun characteristic that captures the personality of each character in the television sets below (i.e. the high performer may have eight arms or a big brain; the big personality may have a top hat and cane to perform with; the low performer may have a large and open mouth with question marks all around; the leader may be standing at the front of a line of people). This is your show, so have fun describing your people.

5. For each character, describe them in a few defining words or phrases—what makes them who they are and how do they impact the whole of the office/sitcom.

Show name: _____

The High Performer

_____
_____
_____
_____
_____

The Big Personality

_____
_____
_____
_____

Figure 5.1   The Sitcom

The Low Performer

The Leader

1. Will people want to watch your sitcom because the characters are funny and work well together or because they are dysfunctional and hilarious?

2. How can you leverage the strengths of the characters to improve your work environment?

3. Do you see how others may view your office from the outside based on the sitcom you have created?

4. What can you do to enhance the culture in your environment through your key characters in order to achieve greater clarity?

You will discover in the following pages the impact drivers or 11 levers we routinely employ for and with our clients. For each, we've provided some descriptions of what it looks like when you are only in compliance with them. We've also given you some steps you can begin with that when pulling that lever with the commitment to drive impact, you will notice it. The real beauty of the drivers is that they are ready, waiting for you to pull, and all you have to do is engage. In fact, most of the levers will look familiar—and most of them are currently employed within your organization. The key here is to understand the impact you can and want to achieve with them.

This is one of the areas as a leader that you have a choice between being compliant and being committed. Where you land on this spectrum goes a far way in the ultimate impact you can drive. The intentionality of impact is real—and so, too, is the leader's role in achieving it. As you reflect on the impact drivers that follow, there is no particular order. Only you can create a hierarchy based on where the opportunities and imbalances in your organization's performance are currently taking place. The balance of your box will guide you as to which levers to pull. These 11 levers together will have a demonstrable impact on moving your organization toward positivity and propelling performance.

THE 11 LEVERS THAT DRIVE IMPACT

Lever: Organizational Audit

Being Compliant/Underperforming

Compliant companies are conducting annual surveys to assess organizational awareness, understanding, and engagement. However, more and more, leaders believe conducting the survey is enough—rarely sharing the results back to their employees in a meaningful way. Employees invest the time, but are not sure their voice is heard. Other companies choose to invest efforts on the front end of the research process by incentivizing employees to participate, rather than the back end where they are genuinely interested in the employee insights and then sharing results.

Being Committed/Creating Impact

1. Standardize a survey establishing a benchmark.

2. Communicate responses with actions (50 percent of the story in this situation is better than nothing).

3. Set up third-party administration and evaluation to encourage acceptance by the workforce.

4. Address gaps and share the expectations to ensure accountability.

Lever: Vision

Being Compliant/Underperforming

Compliant companies and leadership teams set a vision for the organization. However, the vision is rarely articulated clearly, defined, or shared with the organization, or aligned with its mission and values. It is often a lofty set of goals that are disconnected from the organization's core.

Being Committed/Creating Impact

1. Link vision to mission and organization's identity.

2. Define vision and expected outcomes.

3. Use 27 words or fewer to create a vision—bring it to life in "two or three words."

4. Define key phrases of the vision statement with clear outcomes.

Lever: Strategic Plan

Being Compliant/Underperforming

Compliant organizations place emphasis on the creation of an often-robust plan. It becomes a once-every-one-to-three-year exercise, often for compliance or board requirements. The plan, rather than the planning, becomes the focus, leaving the organization with a static document rarely tethered to organizational goals and actions. Many compliant plans have limited accountability measures attached.

Being Committed/Creating Impact

1. Make planning a discipline (over the simple deliverable of a plan).

2. Create structure for monthly, quarterly, and annual updates.

3. Communicate expectations and progress with your organization.

4. Develop cascading accountability.

Lever: Behavioral Alignment

Being Compliant/Underperforming

Compliant organizations believe in their people and invest energy in the furtherance of their values. They use the values in posters and messaging, and many times carry badges listing them. Compliant companies often weight knowledge, skills, and abilities (KSAs) over behaviors in their hiring and development processes. Some companies unintentionally allow competing models across the organization and do not link behaviors and values.

Being Committed/Creating Impact

1. Set clear expectations—identify levels and behaviors.

2. Align behaviors with values.

3. Understand important traditions. (Big *T*'s and Little *t*'s—the big *T*'s are the set-in-stone traditions that cannot change; the little *t*'s are the newer actions that people believe are long-standing traditions.)

4. Educate and engage employees around your values and behaviors: what they mean and what successful actions look like.

5. Integrate values and behaviors into how you hire, evaluate, and develop your people.

Lever: Organizational Structure

Being Compliant/Underperforming

Compliant organizations believe in structure and work to create clarity around the reporting relationships throughout the company. However, in many companies, organizational charts don't match people's roles, responsibilities, or influence. Many organizational charts are constructed on top of an inherited organizational structure creating a "frankenstructure," with little organizational understanding or clarity. Compliant organizations build boxes to fit the people and their skills.

Being Committed/Creating Impact

1. Create structure based on purpose, not people.

2. Align your structure with strategy and your desired outcomes.

3. Communicate the structure.

4. Create pathways for expected growth (succession planning).

Lever: Employee Performance Management
Being Compliant/Underperforming

Compliant organizations work to ensure employee performance through a series of tools, including some among the most sophisticated software programs available. These companies confuse the systems and software with the act of truly driving and measuring employee performance. Some organizations mistake performance management for an annual performance review and traditional top-down processes.

Being Committed/Creating Impact

1. Establish clear goals and expectations aligned with the strategy.

2. Develop a feedback culture providing ongoing coaching and development.

3. Evaluate on values and behaviors, not just KSAs.

4. Conduct 360 Reviews on leadership focused on values and behaviors.

Lever: Reward and Recognition
Being Compliant/Underperforming

Compliant organizations work to recognize and reward employees on a regular basis. There is talk among leadership about recognition and reward, with much of it tied to general performance. Many companies provide end-of-year bonuses based on unclear metrics or overly complex structures. Many of the most compliant companies place greater emphasis on reward over recognition. Other organizations limit their efforts because of budgetary constraints (often not included in the annual budget).

Being Committed/Creating Impact

1. Develop meaningful recognition programs—tie to specific targets and areas.

2. Encourage involvement in the development of the program.

3. Make the process as transparent as possible and ensure leadership's continuing involvement in it.

4. Emphasize recognition of behaviors over results (results are important, too, but the focus here is the behavioral alignment).

5. Ensure the recognition and rewards program is far reaching—touching all levels and all areas of the organization (in other words, it's not just about one group or another, that is, sales or service, but everyone).

Lever: Environmental Design

Being Compliant/Underperforming

Compliant organizations invest in creating an office environment to support their external brand and engagement efforts. They are often well appointed, more generic spaces. These spaces are often disconnected from the culture and more focused on the customer perspective rather than the employee experience. These spaces, which are often less than authentic from an organizational perspective, have generic artwork and some even employ motivational messaging for the back-office employees. This creates inconsistency and a divide in the organization.

Being Committed/Creating Impact

1. Promote the vision, values, and behaviors within the space.

2. Put the organization's identity and culture on display.

3. Leverage the design to affect the way you work.

4. Make periodic changes to keep it fresh and employees engaged and interested.

Lever: Organizational Communication

Being Compliant/Underperforming

Compliant companies place great effort into communications. They have newsletters, videos, and other web-based tools. They focus on delivering the message du jour, rarely linking it to organizational strategies and priorities or taking into account the manner in which it is received by employees. They value communicating over engaging. They focus on different messages to different audiences, often with an obsession on the external customer.

Being Committed/Creating Impact

1. Develop an organizational communication platform with all constituencies identified.

2. Align communications with strategy and culture, not just operations.

3. Create internal focus first.

4. Promote face-to-face communication when possible (that is, no-email day).

Lever: Customer Experience Modeling

Being Compliant/Underperforming

Compliant companies focus on the customer experience with a variety of tools. Many place a heavy emphasis on one or two key touchpoints at the expense of all others. There is a lack of focus on the totality that a touchpoint on a customer, internal or external, will have with the organization. This produces an inconsistent understanding of the customer, an uneven narrative, and an unfulfilled experience.

Being Committed/Creating Impact

1. Identify all touchpoint for customer experiences.

2. Develop a plan for each touchpoint before, during, and after the experience.

3. Identify "100 little things" that can transform a customer experience.

4. Develop a purposeful experience plan targeting a minimum number of changes each quarter.

Lever: Positivity

Being Compliant/Underperforming

Compliant leaders spend time and effort spinning a positive story, regardless of the facts or situation. They go out of their way to incorporate lines and key phrases in memos, presentations, and speeches. Their words and energy can be perceived as disingenuous if not embedded in their actions, organization, or leadership style. Compliant organizations have C-level leaders who embrace positivity while others below them do not. Gratitude is not encouraged or practiced throughout the organization.

Being Committed/Creating Impact

1. Promote and demonstrate gratitude in action.

2. Conduct purposeful and positive exercises—create positive thinking.

3. Create an empowerment culture—purposeful visibility leadership.

4. Encourage and promote health and wellbeing.

Now that we've reviewed all 11 levers and how you can drive impact by being committed to each of them in different ways, we want to build out a couple of them for you to give you some insight into what can be when impact is truly driven.

Let's Pull a Couple Levers

Lever: Behavioral Alignment

Committed Action: Identifying Behavioral Competencies

Behavioral competencies are the mechanisms for norming individual behaviors in a manner that benefits the organization and its capacity to execute on its business strategy. The Association for Talent Development emphasized in 2011 the importance of competencies, stating, "Organizations that understand the characteristics of those who get the best results develop a competitive advantage. They are better positioned to recruit, select, develop, reward, and promote the most successful people. Hence, competencies are an important tool, much like a compass, to find direction in attracting, developing, retaining, and positioning the best, most productive and promotable people. In this regard, competencies are the glue that holds talent management programs together." Identifying and standardizing the right behaviors *for your environment* is a critical step toward achieving an aligned workforce with a commitment to ongoing performance improvement.

To facilitate this, we rely on behavioral competencies. In the early days of Deutser, we were using existing behavioral competency models, but found them to be too general for ensuring clarity. Over time, we developed our own with the understanding that clarity facilitates alignment for the intended destination. Organizations typically rely on knowledge, skills, and abilities as their basis for hiring and evaluating performance, but *in* clarity, there is another level of behavioral competency that sits squarely in the box, meaning: Will this person perform well in this environment, allowing for optimal alignment to execute our business strategy? Or put another way, will they fit into the way we do things around here?

Clients have consistently identified our behavioral competencies as the key that unlocked their previous logjam. These 28 competencies specifically define the basic expectations at every level.

The behavioral competencies are presented to our clients as a card deck of 28 cards. We have measured and identified these as the behaviors of high-performance companies and organizations. No company or individual can successfully implement and focus on all of these. All who experience the cards say that all are important—but the truth is that we can't master all of them—and we for sure can't focus on all of them in our business. So, we start by having the organizational leaders sort through the cards in order to identify five cards as the core behaviors that everyone in the organization must live up to—regardless of their title, tenure, or rank. They are instructed to choose five behaviors that they believe are so important that they are essential to the success or failure of their organization. Only five. Additionally, we then ask them to do another pass through the same card deck and choose five different behavioral competencies for the leadership of the company. This might include some of the core behaviors chosen for all, or it might be that when focused on leadership alone, other factors take precedence. Every company is different, and thus the card selection reflects that uniqueness.

With leadership in mind, your leadership might be focused on as many as 10 total behaviors—five core to all employees and as many as five additional ones for leaders.

These are the core behavioral competencies that they are asked to choose from and that the company will then hire for—evaluate for—develop for—promote for—and even replace for. When we talk about a leader's ability to change the people or change the people, this is where the competencies come into play. You'll find a detailed description of each to give you an accurate understanding of all 28. As you read them, imagine choosing only five that you would adopt throughout your organization to begin to define your outcomes and affect your results. The actual process we go through with companies is very robust, adds creativity, uses a number of tactile objects for engagement, and engages meaningful conversation by company leaders. But, for the purpose of the book and where you are now, this is a straightforward read, choosing those competencies that are most important to you, recognizing the complexity when you can choose only five.

THE DEUTSER BEHAVIORAL COMPETENCIES
Acting with Integrity

Instills mutual trust and confidence; creates a culture that fosters high standards of ethics; behaves in a fair and ethical manner toward others; demonstrates a sense of corporate responsibility and commitment to all stakeholders.

- Behaves in an honest, fair, and ethical manner; leads by example

- Shows consistency in words and actions; follows through on promises and commitments

- Models high standards of ethics and core values
- Takes personal responsibility for correcting problems or issues

Business Acumen

Demonstrates high regard for company profitability and financial strength; continually identifies and exploits business opportunities for revenue and margin contribution.

- Focuses organizational resources on profit and revenue growth opportunities
- Makes decisions that build shareholder value and support the organization's overall strategy
- Applies thoughtful analysis and clear logic when making business decisions
- Understands the interrelatedness of business decisions on the company's value creation

Driving Continuous Improvement

Ongoing commitment to improving the organization's strategy, human capital, systems, and processes; effectively applies appropriate methodologies, tools, and techniques to identify opportunities, implements solutions, and measures the impact.

- Drives change that is focused on increasing the effectiveness and efficiency of the organization to fulfill its strategic objectives
- Develops structured measurement-driven processes that continually review and improve performance

- Takes a systematic approach to the development and implementation of organizational policies and procedures

- Creates an environment in which continuous improvement is valued and welcomed

Inspiring Others

Creates a sense of direction and purpose for employees, helping build excitement and momentum for change; energizes individuals to strive toward a compelling vision of the future by embracing and embodying the organization's values in all aspects of their work.

- Inspires others' commitment to their work and organizational goals

- Helps others see the benefits of doing their job well, for themselves, their customers, and the greater good

- Appropriately rewards and acclaims individuals, teams, and the organization for excellent work

- Acts as a role model; demonstrates integrity and fairness

Leading Change

Demonstrates the ability to bring about strategic change, both within and outside the organization, to achieve desired outcomes to meet organizational goals; capable of establishing and implementing an organizational vision in a continuously changing environment.

- Communicates the vision for change

- Establishes the support elements necessary for the change to be successful

- Effectively makes a case for change by linking it to the business strategy

- Uses creativity to engage and align people with conflicting interests by providing for people's basic needs for achievement, belonging, reward, and recognition

Managing Vision and Purpose

Communicates a compelling and inspired vision; makes the vision sharable by everyone; able to inspire and motivate entire teams or organizations.

- Sets organizational direction; establishes priorities and clarifies goals

- Encourages active participation in pursuing vision and purpose

- Communicates effectively with employees to ensure their actions align with vision and purpose

- Works to ensure an employee's goals are aligned with the organization's vision and purpose

Strategic Thinking

Develops and evaluates every decision and action in light of current and future states; views the organization holistically; conceptualizes complexity and initiates innovative ideas; challenges current ways of thinking.

- Thinks futuristically and embraces visionary thinking

- Focuses on the whole system; views the organization holistically

- Identifies relationships supporting the whole organization and its vision

- Keeps an open mind to new ideas and adapts to changing environments

Working Collectively

Commits to working together as a cohesive team toward a common purpose to achieve the best possible outcome for clients and customers.

- Works toward a shared vision for the organization that includes a common understanding of what we are trying to accomplish and a joint approach to solving problems through agreed-upon actions

- Complies with how success is measured and reported; adheres to the established performance indicators identified; uses outcomes for learning and improvement

- Works with team members through a mutually reinforcing plan of action to achieve the desired goals and outcomes of the organization

- Engages in frequent and structured open communication to build trust, assure mutual objectives, and create common motivation

Working Safely

Understands, encourages, and carries out the principles of integrated safety management; complies with or oversees compliance with safety policies and procedures; completes all required safety training; takes personal responsibility for safety.

- Understands the importance of maintaining a safe work environment; calls attention to things that may pose safety hazards

- Respects and follows safety policies and regulations; takes safety regulations seriously; keeps up to date on safety policies

- Maintains a heightened sense of safety awareness; scans the environment for things that may pose a safety risk; encourages others to use safe and healthy work practices

- Acts cautiously when it comes to things that may affect people's safety and health; does not push people to take risks that could lead to accidents and injuries; reminds people of the importance of safety and health

Problem Solving

Seeks pertinent data and asks the right questions; recognizes what is important and draws on one's knowledge and experience; sees things others do not and knows when to seek out advice from others.

- Undertakes a complex task by breaking it down into manageable parts in a systematic, detailed way

- Thinks of several possible explanations or alternatives for a situation; anticipates potential obstacles and develops contingency plans to overcome them

- Identifies the information needed to solve a problem effectively

- Provides analysis and recommends solutions to problems

Organizing and Planning Work

Defining tasks and milestones to achieve objectives while ensuring the optimal use of resources to meet those objectives.

- Effectively organizes and plans work according to organizational, team, or individual needs

- Defines and prioritizes objectives, anticipates potential obstacles, and makes necessary adjustments

- Efficiently manages time and effectively handles multiple demands and competing deadlines

- Develops plans, scopes of work, and timelines; monitors progress

Managing and Measuring Work

Demonstrates an authentic interpersonal style that engages others and encourages high performance; manages resources to achieve maximum value and efficiency with minimum costs; communicates clearly with co-workers to ensure alignment.

- Accurately estimates resources and time required to complete projects

- Clearly defines and communicates roles and responsibilities; makes sure people are committed to meeting their goals and objectives

- Gives people constructive feedback in a consistent manner

- Holds people equally accountable for meeting performance expectations regardless of background, position, or past performance

Dealing with Ambiguity

Makes sound decisions based on the limited information available at the time, achieving forward progress even under ambiguous circumstances.

- Works effectively with limited or partial information

- Achieves forward progress in the face of poorly defined situations and unclear goals

- Maintains a positive, productive attitude in the face of ambiguous situations

- Takes maximum advantage of information and available resources

Delivering High-Quality Work

Maintains high standards despite pressing deadlines; does work right the first time; corrects own errors; regularly produces accurate, thorough, professional work.

- Performs tasks accurately and thoroughly; double-checks the accuracy of information and work product

- Sets and maintains high performance standards for self and others; makes adjustments to ensure expectations are met and exceeded

- Communicates and reinforces the importance of high work standards and encourages others to hold themselves accountable

- Takes responsibility and stays focused on problems until an effective solution can be found

Team Player

Works collaboratively with others to achieve group goals and objectives.

- Creates synergy within team, departments, and alliances across the organization

- Motivates others and brings team members together to achieve collaborative results

- Facilitates a cooperative approach within the unit and beyond

- Acts in the best interests of the team and the organization; persuades others to act in the same manner

Self-Awareness

Demonstrates the ability to understand one's own thoughts, feelings, and behaviors and recognizes their impact on others.

- Self-regulates emotions and behaviors consistently and independently; manages emotions so as to minimize any negative impact on others.

- Accurately assesses one's strengths and limitations and possesses a well-grounded sense of confidence and optimism

- Demonstrates the ability to use coping mechanisms to deal with difficult or emotional situations

- Seeks and openly accepts feedback from others without being defensive

Managing Teams

Inspires and fosters team commitment and trust; sets goals and priorities, analyzes the group's work methods, and examines the team's decision-making processes in an effort to achieve a common goal.

- Establishes a common focus, including clear and understandable goals, plans of action, and ways to measure success

- Clearly articulates roles and responsibilities for each team member

- Establishes an organizational environment in which individual team members can reflect upon and analyze relationships with other team members

- Encourages the resolution of any conflicts through healthy, professional confrontation, and willingly and openly negotiates necessary changes

Interpersonal Savvy

Notices, interprets, and anticipates others' concerns and feelings; considers and responds appropriately to the needs and feelings of different people in different situations.

- Easily builds lasting, constructive, and mutually beneficial relationships with other individuals and groups

- Interacts with people in a friendly, open, accepting manner; demonstrates politeness and empathy

- Initiates communication and responds to others in a timely, sensitive manner, exhibiting a confident and positive attitude

- Provides constructive criticism and feedback in a positive fashion (for example, honest, timely, non-attacking)

Drive and Energy

Pursues everything with drive, energy, and a need to finish; does not give up before finishing, even in the face of resistance or setbacks; steadfastly pushes self and others for results.

- Sets clear and challenging goals for himself or herself and pursues them with enthusiasm and energy

- Results are achieved through a persistent, focused effort, overcoming obstacles, fatigue, and periods of discouragement

- Follows up regularly on progress and reinforces any movement in the right direction

- Volunteers for difficult tasks or assignments that require a stretch from his or her current capabilities

Developing Talent

Dedicates time and resources to investing in employees; promotes a culture of learning in the workplace; builds processes to support development; invests in his or her own need to learn and develop to motivate development in others.

- Encourages and supports employees using professional development tools such as seminars and workshops; provides employees with tools to assess their personal and professional goals and strengths

- Demonstrates interest in others' career goals; encourages them to fully realize their own potential

- Performs reviews and evaluations to ensure employees are on target and continuing to grow

- Engages in open, constant communication with employees; gives constructive, developmental feedback and advice

Accepting Direction

Accepts and follows instruction in the performance of duties; is receptive to and actively applies coaching and mentoring that is received in a constructive manner.

- Readily accepts and completes assigned responsibilities

- Cooperates willingly and follows specific instructions

- Follows policies and procedures set by a supervisor and the organization

- Continually works to improve performance following constructive criticism or coaching

Building Relationships

Makes good first impression and relates well to all kinds of people; comfortable starting conversations; able to shift style and tone to fit the audience.

- Introduces him- or herself to others; starts conversations; invites others to talk and listens to what they have to say

- Makes a strong, positive first impression; projects personal credibility and confidence

- Relates to all kinds of people regardless of background; finds topics and common interests that he or she can use to build rapport with others

- Chooses words carefully when engaging others; makes a positive impression on others; adjusts style and tone of conversations to fit the audience

Championing Customer Needs

Responds to and anticipates customer needs and requests; is always courteous to customer and considers the customer's needs when making decisions.

- Places high priority on customer needs and concerns; calls attention to issues that affect customer satisfaction; views things from the perspective of the customer

- Actively monitors customer satisfaction; informs people regarding customer service levels and trends related to customer satisfaction

- Defends customer interests and goals; acts as an advocate for the customer

- Encourages people to think about the customer when making decisions; reminds people that customer service is everyone's responsibility

Communicating Effectively

Conveys ideas clearly and succinctly; tailors the message to the audience, delivering the information in a manner that is accurate and compelling.

- Delivers information to the listener in an interesting and compelling manner; engages the audience

- Expresses ideas and information in a clear and concise manner; focuses on critical information and leaves out unnecessary details; provides effective responses to questions

- Tailors message to fit the interests and needs of the audience; focuses on relevant topics; uses appropriate vocabulary and terminology given the background of the audience

- Uses appropriate language, grammar, and pronunciation; easy to understand

Delivering and Receiving Feedback

Delivers, seeks out, and effectively uses feedback; considers all feedback valuable; delivers and responds to feedback in a positive manner.

- Views feedback and criticism as valuable and useful information; reacts to feedback in a positive, constructive manner

- Changes behavior based on feedback when appropriate

- Seeks feedback; encourages others to do the same

- Delivers feedback in a respectful, encouraging manner

Demonstrating Initiative

Works independently to solve problems; looks for opportunities to take on responsibility and takes thoughtful risks; effectively takes action on new and ongoing initiatives, objectives, and solutions to problems to gain sought-after results.

- Identifies what needs to be done and takes action before being asked or before the situation requires it

- Does more than what is normally required in a situation

- Seeks out others involved in a situation to learn their perspectives

- Identifies and leverages appropriate resources to any potential obstacles

Engaging the Workforce

Empowers the workforce in its decision making and actions; listens to and supports workforce in overcoming barriers; encourages workforce to see its work as critical to the organization; builds community and trust.

- Engages in and encourages active feedback and communication

- Ensures individuals' alignment with the company's goals, and that they understand where they fit into the bigger picture

- Builds relationships with employees to ensure trust

- Develops talents and skills of employees for continuous improvement; offers opportunities for job advancement

Passionate About Your Work

Believes his or her work makes a real difference; commits daily to every task with the understanding of each task's larger significance; commits to his or her goals and achieves them.

- Understands his or her success is tied to the success of the company; understands the link between organizational goals and personal goals

- Believes in the importance of his or her work and how it will contribute to things he or she cares deeply about

- Aligns day-to-day actions to longer-term goals and strategies

- Inspires others by his or her actions to achieve their goals

Now that you've considered the 28 behavioral competencies in our library and the role they play in your organization, use the exercise in Figure 5.2 to create your organization's core and leadership model.

The Right Fit

Clarity never just happens. It is desired, planned for, earned, and must be nurtured and practiced. Driving common-valued behaviors brings benefit to the whole. Creating core behavioral competencies communicates a type of organizational social contract. Behavioral competencies allow companies to more easily see when their purposeful culture is shifting and where they need to direct attention, focus, and resources. These competencies bring the workforce together and cultivate trust, respect, and commitment, and provide a common language and understanding within which to examine contributions and value differences. They engage every employee at every level in shared opportunities to bring their unique contribution forward to achieve the desired goals and dreams of the organization.

While every company is unique, we continue to see variations of the same issues in multiple places. When it comes to talent and hiring, many companies hire based on an applicant's knowledge, skills, and abilities. They place great value on their skills and past performance. This is an important component of hiring, but for the most successful companies, it is not the one determinate of a highly productive future employee.

We were brought into a high-performing, highly skilled company in the service industry that was experiencing a sharp decline in revenue. We studied every relevant aspect of their business and found that the performance decline was directly related to their hiring practices. A large number of long-time employees left the company, several of whom retired or went on to leadership positions at other companies. These employees were replaced with some of the most technically proficient, highly skilled professionals in the world, who had years of experience. Yet, what we learned is that these individuals, while having the knowledge, skills, and abilities to successfully complete the job, did not have the same can-do attitude, customer-facing skills, or other key behaviors their predecessors had that made them so successful in their duties. Almost immediately after the company adopted a hiring practice, which included behavioral interviewing built on their competencies, the company experienced a return to their previous performance standards. This same situation has played out in academia, where a great teacher at one school or college is

Building a Behavioral Competency Model

Using the Deutser Behavioral Competency Library, you will be asked to identify five core and five leadership behavioral competencies that are unique to your company.

┌──────── DEUTSER BEHAVIORAL COMPETENCY LIBRARY ────────┐

Accepting Direction	Inspiring Others
Acting with Integrity	Interpersonal Savvy
Building Relationships	Leading Change
Business Acumen	Managing + Measuring Work
Championing Customer Needs	Managing Teams
Communicating Effectively	Managing Vision + Purpose
Dealing with Ambiguity	Organizing + Planning Work
Delivering High-Quality Work	Passionate About Your Work
Delivering + Receiving Feedback	Problem Solving
Demonstrating Initiative	Self-Awareness
Developing Talent	Strategic Thinking
Driving Continuous Improvement	Team Player
Drive + Energy	Working Collectively
Engaging the Workforce	Working Safely

Figure 5.2   Building A Behavioral Competency Model

Step One: Identifying Core Behaviors

- From the list on the previous page, write in the five behaviors that all employees need to exhibit at a high level in order for your organization to be successful.
- Rate each behavior according to the 5-point scale below on how well employees currently exhibit those behaviors.

TOP 5 CORE BEHAVIORS

	NEVER EXHIBITS	RARELY EXHIBITS	SOMETIMES EXHIBITS	REGULARLY EXHIBITS	ALWAYS EXHIBITS
1. _____	1	2	3	4	5
2. _____	1	2	3	4	5
3. _____	1	2	3	4	5
4. _____	1	2	3	4	5
5. _____	1	2	3	4	5

Step Two: Identifying Leadership Behaviors

- From the Deutser library, write in the five behaviors that leadership needs to exhibit at a high level for your organization to be successful.
- Rate each behavior according to the 5-point scale below on how well employees currently exhibit those behaviors.

TOP 5 LEADERSHIP BEHAVIORS

	NEVER EXHIBITS	RARELY EXHIBITS	SOMETIMES EXHIBITS	REGULARLY EXHIBITS	ALWAYS EXHIBITS
1. _____	1	2	3	4	5
2. _____	1	2	3	4	5
3. _____	1	2	3	4	5
4. _____	1	2	3	4	5
5. _____	1	2	3	4	5

FOLLOW-UP REFLECTION

Does your organization have a company-wide behavioral competency model? Explain.

_____

_____

_____

_____

_____

In what ways does your company promote the behaviors and hold employees accountable?

_____

_____

_____

_____

_____

not successful at another. It is also true with executives who are hired for their success at one company, but only have the knowledge set of the "way things are done" at their old company, which does not translate well to the new company's cultural expectations.

LEVER: ENVIRONMENTAL DESIGN

Committed Action: Defining Your Environment

So much of our focus in clarity is supporting the people who work for us and who are doing the work on the frontlines to help us achieve our goals. The behavioral competencies are an important impact driver for us that when leveraged with other drivers, like environmental design, can exponentially expand our results. We find this lever to be one of the best to elevate employee engagement. When people who spend 40 or more hours a week together in the same space get to help inform the creation of the space, it brings together intention, vision, problem solving, and a healthy dose of fun. It allows everyone to feel like part of something great that is shared and experienced by all. By using your sixth side of the box, you will extend your intentions to those who visit you and rely on functional spaces within which to interact. With decentralized physical workspaces today, the integration of new technology in an office redesign can facilitate both efficiency and flexibility between teams, clients, and offices and closes the physical gap between people working together.

Defining Deutser

We always said that we believed the office environment was important. We always had very nice offices decorated with beautiful carpets, nice furniture, and artwork to support the space. In hindsight, we were compliant with our space. Only when we identified and defined our behavioral expectations and created "our way," were we able to create an absolutely committed environment in every way. We had finally found the right space for our growing group, a space that we could build out to our own specifications and one that would allow us to be intentional about every decision that would affect the environment where we created our work and partnered with our clients.

Everything in our office was intentional. It was important to us that every decision had a story and that our physical space had meaning. Our full staff worked together to co-create the ideas that became our working environment and where we would all collaborate daily. This was not just about design and making a statement, which it does; it is about fundamentally rethinking how we work and interact and how we insert new ways to drive productivity and performance. Let me take you on a tour of Deutser.

The Library

This was one of the first areas that defined Deutser in alignment with our belief in the importance of learning agility and learning from experience, one of our competencies. Our library rests on beautiful high-gloss-shelved bookcases that you'll find as you enter our office. These shelves are filled with leading business books, with the left section representing strategy and the right section containing our creative and design books. The center section that connects them is where we shelve our culture and leadership books. This provides a tangible testament to the unbreakable link that culture and leadership provides companies.

The Clarity Jumble

Our office has a beautiful view easily seen through large windows, drenched with sunlight and a vibrant blue sky. People were a bit skeptical when I decided to partially obscure the view by installing a large sculpture in our entrance that featured enormous white letters that spell one word: CLARITY. I wanted there to be no mistake about what our mission is. However, there is a twist to the sculpture as the letters are jumbled so that the person reading it has to focus on its meaning. There are many messages embedded in this 10-foot wide sculpture, the first is that clarity is often in front of us even if it is sometimes difficult to see. Also, I wanted every employee to pass by that sculpture and embrace why we're here. The unexpected intrusion of the word often prompts visitors and clients to understand that we are serious about Clarity! Many have mentioned that it immediately both inspires and energizes them to find what they came here for: clarity about their own business conundrums.

In a Sea of Ambiguity

When we started thinking about our floors, we knew we wanted the walk through the office to have some tone and texture to it. The light gray coloring of the tile, carpet, and flooring is designed to represent the ambiguity and gray matter executives walk through and work to navigate every day. The pattern of the tile subtly represents the waves of the ocean, which is designed to remind us of the ups and downs and constant change that organizations and individuals face.

Our Colors

Throughout the office you'll find the Deutser colors—the gray, which is Pantone Cool Gray 10, represents the gray areas that leaders must deal with every day. Our Deutser Red is a specially formulated color that represents the vibrancy and purposeful nature of solution. These colors remind us of our core message.

The Gray Area

This room features chalkboard walls with powerful, culture-focused graffiti graphics drawn in chalk and a low-hanging chandelier that allows for paper handwritten notes to be clipped to it. This room helps infuse us with creativity and reminds us to not get too attached to any one idea as the drawings we enjoy one day may be replaced with something else in the coming days.

The Blank Space

This is a stark white room that provides a mind respite and a reset to neutral. There are white glass surfaces filling every wall and a special white conference table that doubles as a Ping Pong table, with the net properly placed in the middle to reinforce the hurdles and necessary exchanges that organizations must deal with every day. Just by its name and clean construct (without the multicolored Dry-Erase Marker drawings and words on the glass boards), it encourages free, unfiltered thought and creativity.

The Collaboration Stations

As you walk down our hallway, you'll find offices on both sides along with a series of three standing-height tables in the center. These are our collaboration stations where staff are encouraged to meet in the middle for purposeful discussions. Each station has a different intention. The first station (topped with a whimsical display of colored pens) is our "color your world" station, which encourages any and all colorful conversations. The second station (with a set of gratitude cards, a set of positivity cards, and a set of happiness cards, each with blank backs for personal thoughts to be placed in an oversized old glass jar) is known for "grounded conversations," which encourages grateful, focused conversation. The third station (appropriately topped with all different-sized Stickie notes and Sharpie markers) is for "sticky conversations," where we meet to hash out sticky, more challenging issues. Much like our Huemanize Mind Map in Chapter 4, these stations prompt a mindset where the act of meeting there informs intention.

The Fighting Wall of Snacks

This wall of easily accessible and well-stocked snacks encourages choice by offering both healthy and unhealthy snacks. Regardless of your food choice, there is always camaraderie and some quick sustenance to be found.

The Zen Room

This room speaks to clarity of mind and intention as much as any space in the office. It offers a special retreat for employees and guests, giving us a place to pause, center ourselves, practice daily morning meditations, and connect with what is meaningful. There is a wall with a special wallpaper we created with an image of a mandala, appropriately called Trajectory, to encourage focus and to increase the trajectory of thought and expectation for the day. The room also has Deutser Red meditation pillows covering the floor, a live wall of plants and herbs, a tabletop waterfall, a diffuser with essential oils, and anything else we can add to support the clarity of thought for each of our people.

The Back Wall

Remember the wall we told you about in Chapter 3 that originally read "The only lines we care about are our clients' growing bottom lines"? Well, when our client challenged us on the message and intentionality of it, we did start over. We designed an interesting piece of art—a raw, eight-foot piece of wood with a message routed in the wood. The message captures the essence of who we are and what we do: save lives, increase performance, reduce risk, increase happiness, decrease accidents, improve results, drive the bottom line, unite people, reduce suicides, target consumers, change lives, and so on.... At the bottom of the wall, is embedded the only color on the wall, red letters that say, "Delivering Clarity."

As you can see, environmental design tied to culture is an important element of organizations in every industry. Everything in our space affects the way we work and has fundamentally changed the level of collaboration, creativity, and performance. That is true for many of the organizations that we work with as well.

You Can't Say No

When people visit our space, they get excited and want to replicate some of the elements that they can convince us to "squeeze into their box." It's not every day that the president of a former First Lady's not-for-profit office calls with a request to create the organization's brand and then design the office environment around it. Our first response was that we were honored, but we had served in the function of decorators for only two previous projects, both of which were large industrial spaces. The response was the same: "We want our brand and your taste on our walls." We were clear that this was not a cause (literacy) or family you say no to. Through our process, we were able to easily get to the essence of their mission and built not only the box but the desired experience for each employee, volunteer, and visitor. Instead of highlighting the name of the organization so all visitors could easily identify the space from the exterior hallway, we created three Andy Warhol–like images of the former First Lady to hang as the centerpiece of the office's entry. While unusual to take such an elegant, sophisticated, and distinctive lady and showcase her with red, orange, and yellow hair, the images set the tone and created the youthful and relevant presence that defined the organization. We then wallpapered one of the prominent corners of the office, which was visible from the entry area, with an image of a stack of books and a small child sitting on the floor reading. Our point was made—reading is cool and is something that kids are doing all the time. The larger "bullpen area" for the bevy of daily volunteers was appointed with wall-to-wall images of adults and children reading to each other as well as famous quotes on the importance of reading. The experience we collectively created reinforced the importance of every wall and every corner to tell a story and create meaning. This forward-thinking organization understood that volunteers had a choice and that by creating an environment that supported their passion, they would be able to not only attract more volunteers, but keep them more satisfied and connected to the cause. Their understanding and commitment to space again reinforces that the experience must be as purposeful for the employee as it is for the volunteer and end user or customer.

A Community of People

One of the most purposeful spaces we have collaborated on was for an organization whose sole focus is community. In fact, *community* is in its name. The visionary leader of the organization wanted a space that eliminated work silos, created equality of every position, reinforced collaboration, changed meeting structures, and represented the extraordinary reach of the organization. A tall task, indeed. The architect, thinking about the perceived limited resources of the organization, designed a box that looked closer to the interior of a prison than an open, collaborative, professional, and highly creative space. The original design placed emphasis on the front of the house versus the back of the house. Every accoutrement (and decorating dollar) was designed for the customer and the front space. We were asked to inject creativity and community into the space. Since this office was meant to focus on community, we shifted the focus to the whole of the office with greater concentration on the back. We cut the front customer conference room in half, making one a private living room and the other a welcoming kitchen environment so that client families could meet with the staff in a comfortable, somewhat familiar environment. There were the traditional conference rooms for board meetings and community groups, but the space in the back defined the office. Every employee, regardless of title, had the same-sized office, each with outward-facing glass walls and doors, to encourage, and even force, collaboration and community building. In the back, we created a "community gathering space" with interesting furniture groupings to encourage community conversations; large 4-foot × 4-foot glass game boards with word search (words included key organizational outcomes and values), with connect-the-dots (reinforcing the organization's role in the community), and other nontraditional games. We created a "Community Pinterest" pinup wall where members of the staff cover a wall with community pictures, messages, or dreams, and the centerpiece of the space, which showcased nine television sets in a square grid. Eight of the televisions were connected to a live feed from eight areas across the community and the middle television had an inspirationally focused message of the organization's role in convening and connecting. The space transformed work behaviors, increased productivity, and drove retention and employee performance across the organization.

11 Levers, Unlimited Impact

As leaders, we employ these powerful, business-changing levers on a regular basis. But as we have explored, simply employing them does not correlate to success. It is the intentionality, whether we are simply compliant or truly committed, that is tied to them that determines the measure of impact they ultimately make on our companies. As much as any practice in the book, these drivers require a discipline to dig deeper and not accept the surface or previously accepted approach. It is easy to dismiss these by saying "we already do this," but it is different when you execute them in a concerted, committed way with genuine clarity of purpose. When the right levers are pulled with the right force, the fusion of information and engagement creates a chain reaction that catalyzes all dimensions of performance.

CHAPTER 6

The Energy of Alignment

O ften in dysfunction, devolution, and downright deceit, people are forced into opposition and rush to polarize. During the drive to polarity, there is a lot of energy kicked up. That energy can take shape as chaos, disorganization, disruption, and distraction. Companies funnel that energy into communicating, retraining, problem solving, mediation, reorganization of teams or departments, and so on. In between two polarized points lies ambivalence. Ambivalence is a form of dropping out, or "keeping your head low" that brings with it other issues and problems such as mediocrity, status quo, flat results, an unwillingness or fear to try, entropy, and such. Mediocrity can become walled off as some sort of kink or benign tumor in an organization that straddles "safe" status in the middle. The reality is that an organization can last for years under the influence of ambiguity while chaos and disorganization usually call out for more immediate attention. Ambivalence can, over time, create rot. Clarity is one of the best antidotes to ambivalence because it moves the needle. Employees, teams, and leaders are forced from the sideline into participation. Ambivalence governs the wait-and-see responses from employees that can cripple a department, an objective, or even a new initiative. When the results are "good" or "fine," you're operating in ambivalence. Fine is "good enough." Good is a pathway to a prolonged "okay." Good as an outcome or destination is lacking and ultimately destructive.

Clarity trumps good. It trumps it every time and in every way. Clarity is the exhale in tension that allows you to regroup and get someplace better. Clarity is always about going back to the core—who we are, what we do, and how we do it. It is our foundation and place from which we act and respond to the changing worlds that we enter on a seemingly regular basis.

Alignment depends on exchange. There must be a willingness up and down the structure to exchange energy (conversation, data, observation, and insights, and flat-out brilliance). Alignment is all about a different level of engagement and energy. It isn't about right and wrong; it isn't about only one way to do things. Alignment becomes the power source in an environment in which we are clear about what we're doing and why, what our role is in the shape of what's to come, and even clear about what our reward will be for bringing more than "good enough" to the table. Alignment occurs when people are acknowledged for putting themselves out there and yet clear about what the boundaries are.

Most of us knew from our own early education that being part of a team or production meant you couldn't miss practice, a rehearsal, a game, or a performance—the show always had to go on, and one missing member from any team could wreak havoc. So, short of broken legs, laryngitis, or the death of a loved one, we knew we had to be there. There was no option—our teammates, fellow castmembers, and fellow students were counting on us. There is a spirit and vibrancy that is contagious and expected. Alignment generates energy that propels us to do our part, which brings us into constant awareness that our part is essential to the overall process and the whole of success. Otherwise, we wouldn't have a job there. Alignment encourages us to bring our full being and our best efforts into the situation. When leadership is engaged in the practice of alignment, every employee knows and understands his or her role, appreciates and relies on each other, and can see equally when the workload has exceeded capacity and adjustments need to be made. A 2016

Harvard Business Review article reported how studies have found that "100% of companies with higher-performing employees have a formal linkage between corporate and individual goals. *Alignment is a two-way street which begins at/extends from both levels (top-down and bottom-up) and intersects in the middle.*" Clarity facilitates, encourages, supports, and sustains alignment. In Chapter 4, you looked at the purposeful act of clearing mis-alignments. That clearing process eases the way for alignment to happen more organically while operating in clarity.

EMPLOYEE ENGAGEMENT INCREASES WITH ALIGNMENT

As leaders, our experience tells us when things are working well for an organization and when they are not. Often, when they are working well, things tend to be in alignment. The challenge is often taking the time to slow down and acknowledge what we are seeing and feeling, and then work to distinguish what it really is. We often have a sense of when and where things are aligned and misaligned in our own companies. But, the demands on our time and attention can easily distract us from a true exploration of what is happening. All leaders get distracted and side tracked at some point, but the great one find a way to rally back to what is most important. In the case below, it was survival.

From our first meeting with this industry-defining tech-nology company, the energy was palpable. The dark, gray walls, locked conference room doors, 1980s-style table, and dimly lit space gave us the first clue that the company had significant alignment challenges. Then, their team entered the room, dressed similarly in black polo shirts featuring the company logo emblazoned on their chests. Everyone was professional, but guarded—consistent with the environment. Then, the conversation began and it became clear that at this company, there was the leadership team ... and everyone else. Yes, they all shared the morbidly dark perspective, dour outlook, and gray walls. But, that was all they shared. It was clear and purposeful that there was a divide. Even the language used by members of the leadership team to describe the workforce, and each other, demonstrated a split organization. There was little to no agreement or flow of positive energy throughout the organization, as evidenced by the Clarity Performance Index, which showed dismal performance and disparate views of the company, depending on position, specifically between leader and line-level employee. Worse, the performance scores specific to employee engagement indicated there were more detractors in their workforce than promoters. The research showed that there was no alignment and in many ways, even less hope for the overall health of the company.

The employees recognized the company's obsession with day-to-day operations and the lack of a real long-range strategy and any focus or belief in the company's culture. The leaders acknowledged that they could not focus on culture because they believed it was not something that would affect the performance of the people or the organization. It was made very clear to us that "culture" was a dirty word. In their minds, addressing the company's culture was reserved for soft and fuzzy exercises that held little merit. This company, facing significant financial pressure to remain viable, was not at a time in its history when they were willing to deviate from the tried and true, even though the tried and true was exactly the strategy that led the company to the brink of financial chaos. Little had been done during the previous "dark years," a time when the company was bleeding cash and focused on issues not directly affecting the operations of the business. There were leadership squabbles, legal battles, and a company slowly moving backward. There was no invest-ment back into the company or into employee development. Half joking, one of the leaders described his colleague's idea of motivating employees was to "prop them up at their desks with an IV drip of coffee." And, the atmosphere proved his point.

It was clear that every side of their box needed to be rethought. Even in all the disarray, there were glimmers of hope buried in their narrative and in their eyes. We could see that there was a willingness and deep desire to be something different, although they made it clear that they would fight us every step of the way. It was just who they were.

The alignment effort started with the box. We began by addressing the direction, perhaps the most contentious side for them because of the years of disagreement, by building a robust strategic plan with cascading accountability from the CEO of the company to the management team to the line-level employees. This may seem basic, and it is, but this was a transformational moment for the company. It forced leadership out of its "battle mentality" and allowed them to breathe and envision something outside of their current reality. It provided a mental break, and the planning process gave them permission to reorient their minds into a future state that resonated with all employees. The strategy allowed the company to balance its operational focus with its future vision.

One of the imperatives from the plan was to create a new, appropriate identity for the organization and its leaders. As a tech-savvy company, the brand needed to immediately connote innovation, modernity, and professionalism. They changed the narrative of the company and eliminated black from the color palette—and their daily dress. The intended message to employees and customers was that this was a new day at the company. A bright future lay ahead.

With these "quick wins" from the strategic plan established, and a better understanding of how to apply our research, their perspective began to change. Through the process of change, they began to recognize the need for balance between the strategic systems (direction and operations) and the culture systems (people and engagement) to allow the necessary flow of energy between the two to work. That energy flow was obviously a missing key component to exorcising the negativity that pervaded the office and operations.

While it took quite awhile to convince them that the ROI of an employee engagement program was worth their time and resources, they reluctantly acquiesced when they realized there was a tangible outcome to their efforts, and everything was backed by real science. The program soon took on a life of its own and manifested itself with the development of a full competency model and new values that described the company's way of working. They redesigned processes and protocols to become more employee-centric. They redesigned the office space and introduced activities to encourage their values. They went from the proverbial bad guys to the visionary, collaborative, high-tech leaders they aspired to be. Leaders were revered for their willingness to do what was right and best for the company.

Most of all, they changed attitudes about the people on the frontlines—understanding and accepting that they were the ultimate determiners of the company's performance. They proved themselves right, and positive energy could be felt throughout the company. Employees regularly talked about the changes and in follow-up research, noted, "The energy felt different"; "Something was different in the air"; and "I can't describe what I feel. The environment just feels better." (See Figure 6.1.) The next time we tested employee engagement, it had significantly improved, and the profits for the company mirrored the gains in the employee engagement scores. The energy on the inside of an organization not only affects those inside, but those on the outside, too. And to the leaders effecting the change, it felt good

ENERGY OBSTRUCTION GRID

Rank the frequency and intensity of each circuit breaker, based on how it interrupts your work productivity flow overall. Then, plot each one (using its symbol) on the grid below.

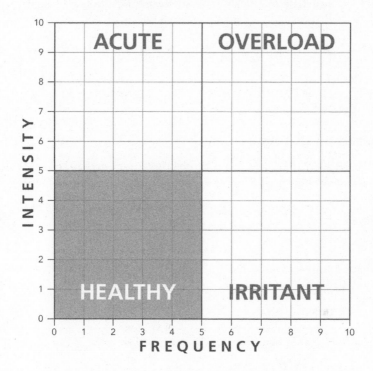

LIST OF CIRCUIT BREAKERS

(A) AMBIVALENCE

(B) BOREDOM/MONOTONY (LACK OF INSPIRATION + HIGHER THOUGHT)

(CF) CONFLICT

(CL) CLUTTER (MENTAL, ORGANIZATIONAL, PHYSICAL DISORDER)

(D) DOUBT (LACK OF BELIEF)

(F) FEAR

(IN) INFERENCE

(L) LABELING

(OV) OVERCONFIDENCE

(PD) PHYSICAL DEPLETION

(RE) RESOURCES (FINANCES, ETC.)

(S) STRESS

Figure 6.1   Energy Obstruction Grid

Quadrant Terms Defined

IRRITANT (HIGH FREQUENCY, LOW INTENSITY) We tend to ignore, but has the potential of derailing performance over time.

ACUTE (LOW FREQUENCY, HIGH INTENSITY) Impossible to ignore, needs immediate intervention or will derail performance.

OVERLOAD (HIGH FREQUENCY, HIGH INTENSITY) Clear and present danger, must actively seek a plan to combat.

HEALTHY (LOW FREQUENCY, LOW INTENSITY) Manageable, part of the equilibrium of life.

Obstruction Quadrants

WHAT'S THE SOURCE? Identify one circuit breaker from each of the energy obstruction quadrants.

List one or two steps you can take to move the circuit breaker into the healthy quadrant.

OVERLOAD _____

1. _____

2. _____

ACUTE _____

1. _____

2. _____

IRRITANT _____

1. _____

2. _____

knowing that they were leading change and making a difference not only to their company, but their employees.

As leaders, we must recognize the daily impediments that surround us and impede our progress. We must also take time to understand if those roadblocks or circuit breakers are real or if they are manufactured in our minds. When we can take the time to understand that we have control over our minds and what we allow to influence us, positively or negatively, we can eliminate wasted energy and lost time. The Energy Obstruction Grid illustrates where energy is being limited, and can lead us to activate our true potential.

CLARITY ALIGNS INTENTION WITH PURPOSE

One of the valuable changes that is made more effortless in clarity is alignment. A renowned prep school brought our team in when a scathing, vitriolic letter about political correctness and the perceived changing values of the school, written by a parent, was shared with a friend. This person then forwarded the email to a small group of friends, and within 48 hours, it took hold on social media and quickly circled the world in a viral feeding frenzy. The fallout was so fierce that every perceived fringe group in the letter self-identified themselves as the reason the parent wrote the letter. It ripped at the fabric of the institution and called into question even its most basic truths. In fact, the reaction was so severe in select social circles that some believed that the very future of the school was in jeopardy. We quickly saw that the entire organization was out of alignment—teachers against the administration, parents against teachers, and administrators against any of a host of concerns, real and perceived, relating to race, ethnicity, religion, sexual orientation…you name it…and every group was split by their own agenda. They all viewed the school through the lens of meeting only their own group's respective needs. We studied each group. Each identified themselves as the one under attack. Most interestingly, the students were, for the most part, on the sidelines, until as the students voiced, "the adults brought us (the students) into the dialog." Fingers were pointing in every direction except for back at the person pointing. Chaos prevailed.

Our view of clarity involved getting to the core to seek an understanding far deeper than the issues on the surface of the organization and on the tongues of the constituents. We chose to focus on the identity of the school and chose not to study the numerous problems mentioned by the various warring groups. Our approach with each person interviewed was to look at the school on its best day—how it operated, the values it brought—and so on. We talked only about positive value and the differentiation that had made it unique for the past century. This data very clearly showed there was misalignment based on the various groups. People felt violated because they believed they had a social contract with the school that had certain perceived understandings in it that weren't being honored. But instead of a feeling of inclusiveness and exemplary attention, it was clear that factions of the school had devolved into haves and have-nots—liberals and conservatives—and just about any other group that was polarized on the basis of self-identity and unwanted labels. Each group was defending their own agenda and assuming a social contract with the school to provide for it.

What we found validated that there wasn't an ulterior agenda by any of these groups, but instead, legitimate differences. The school board was initially taken aback by the presentation of the research and data collected. It was raw. They feared that the reality of the different perspectives and belief systems, which weren't valued or understood by the various constituents, would split the school apart. Parents took issue with elements of the approach to religious tolerance, diversity, and political correctness. Faculty had an issue with the lack of attention, focus, and dialog on a host of evolving values coming to the forefront of not only the school's psyche, but that of the country as a whole. Students felt disenfranchised because adults were thrusting their opinions on them.

So, alignment started with the school. What clarity brought was that the school itself stood for something—and that something had endured for more than a century. Clarity also brought the realization that they would likely lose some faculty, students, possibly a board member and even philanthropic support. Clarity prepared them for what was necessary, and they became okay with that outcome. They had what few organizations have—a board leader absolute in his commitment to lead his board and his administrative leaders with facts, direction, values, and purpose. Together, we instituted ways that each group could know, "We hear you; now hear us." The school offered a grounding point with which all could become aligned around what they stood for and what they believed in. For the first time since the letter became known throughout the world, emotion was removed from the discussion.

Once the issues were clearly defined and focus shifted to the school they all shared, they finally had a social contract that was purposeful rather than accidental. Alignment allowed them to see how they were alike rather than being so torn about how they were different. Now all could accept the new paradigm: If you knew you were *in* and a part of the school, you knew what you were in *for*. A shared passion for academic excellence once again brought energy to the process of learning rather than so much energy being spent on defending and protecting identity and acceptance. The result was obvious as the organization not only exhaled together, it improved their outcomes across every key performance metric by more than 30 percent. The performance continued to improve year after year for three consecutive years, demonstrating the power of an aligned institution with a strong, committed leader.

ALIGNMENT ALLOWS ENERGY TO FLOW

Energy flows through an organization at all times. Depending on timing and circumstances, that energy takes many forms: It can be stagnant, it can be infectious and positive, or it can be filled with negativity and be stifling. Regardless of the energy form, it has a definitive impact on business and employee performance, especially in challenging economic environments.

When we worked with a publicly traded company in an industry rife with economic challenges, the competitive landscape was littered with layoffs and uncertainty. For more than two years, highly respected competitors were laying people off and cutting costs to remain viable. This cast a pall on the industry and the many towns affected by the layoffs, as well as the businesses that serviced these companies. The leadership team we worked with refused to negatively affect the lives of its workforce with layoffs. They had managed their business and cash in a manner to allow a much more forgiving approach. Yet, as the economic environment continued to get worse, it was clear that the current plan to protect all workers was no longer a viable business plan. The leadership understood that they could only protect the whole of the company with efficiencies, rethought customer agreements, and a reduction in force. This was the pathway to not only survival, but sustainability. Based on the economic environment and competitive landscape, the workforce already knew that action had to be taken.

Silence and inaction stifled energy throughout the organization. Individuals who worked together for years, if not decades, began to pull away from each other. Innovation and ideation stopped. The workforce was waiting for what they knew had to eventually come. After holding out for more than two-plus years versus their competitors, the leadership took action to reduce less than 5 percent of the workforce. They viewed this through one of the most compassionate, employee-focused lenses we have seen in three decades of business. Their focus was rightly on the individual lives that composed the 5 percent. Our focus was on those employees, but equally important, it was on the more than 95 percent continuing on with the company who would be the future.

We knew that how we treated the 5 percent and what we did to communicate and engage the workforce before, during, and after would define the culture going forward. We knew that we needed to reorient the energy and create a measure of transparency and positivity that was nonexistent. We chose to "sound the alarm"—telling the employees several months before the cuts that they were coming, sharing the process and the exact date they would be complete, explaining the landscape and assuring the company that each person, regardless of their employment status, would be taken care of to the best of the company's ability. The leadership also explained that the workforce would always be told well in advance of any future changes to the company and workforce—in short, they connected through trust and assured employees by both communication and action that they could be confident that they would never be blindsided by the company's action.

Yes, it is easier to make the cuts and inform those affected. But, it is not the fair way for those who entrust their careers to the company. The result was the disappointment you would expect, but there was a gratitude and appreciation that was unexpected. The CEO received multiple phone calls, emails, and handwritten letters thanking him for the humanistic approach he took, even from multiple old-timers at the company who lost their jobs. They understood the environment and respected the company for taking action in the manner it did. It restarted the positive flow of energy and created an aligned workforce determined to stick together and redefine their future. The 95 percent was protected and became even more passionate and engaged advocates for the company and the leadership.

Alignment Supports Safety

Organizations affect energy in many ways, often by how they communicate, lead, engage, and make decisions. Energy is absolutely intertwined with culture, with both directly and indirectly affecting each other. In working with organizations focused on improving their safety, we have experienced measurable improvement by reorienting the leadership around a unique safety model and alternative nomenclature. Our model relies on leadership forming the wide base of the foundation of the pyramid (not the top as in many safety models), with layers of ideology, values, belief system, patterns of behavior, and engagement stacking one on top of the other until we reach the peak, composed of clearly and consistently articulated expectations. This creates a more natural flow of energy throughout the organization and helps to align the people and their safety practices. With our model, leadership creates expectations and behaviors for the workforce to live up to what is in perfect alignment with the other crucial cultural layers that exist in any company. Our work and subsequent results validate that the behavior-based, instead of rule-based, approach linked with the organization's understanding that positive change is the expectation, is fundamental to positively shifting safety performance. In short, the psychology matters—in the choice of words, in how leaders are perceived, and in the application of positive psychology. In fact, working with one of the world's foremost experts and research teams in positive psychology, we have developed a safety assessment which demonstrates in each company the inextricable link between safety, positivity, and clarity. Positivity amplifies the power grid and adds stimulation to intention. We have shown that employees will change behaviors when they believe that they can and when they are supported through an aligned environment. Clarity connects the circuitry of the power grid.

As consultants, we are all trained to think, or at least say, all of our clients are the best. But in reality, it is the clients who allow and encourage the best work that are among our favorites. These clients are in clarity, and when not, are determined in their pursuit of it. One client in particular relishes the debate and challenge that inevitably occurs in relation to their business. The debate can be fierce, but because safety is a critical component of their business, we understand that the wrong solution can contribute to the death of one of their employees or customers. This is always a fine line and one that outsiders might imagine would be more obvious, but in certain businesses, misalignments can be deadly. This client believes that zero accidents and zero incidents in a highly visible industry with many moving parts is not only achievable, but the only acceptable outcome. This is not a sales gimmick, but rather a deep-seated belief and expectation.

When they came to us to develop a zero program—what is now becoming a ubiquitous exercise for many in the oil and gas and industrial services industries—they wanted not just a program or initiative, but a fundamental change in mindset. They understood that regardless of the words on paper or on posters, it was the reorientation of the employees' belief system that was the key. They understood that by infusing positivity and the belief that zero accidents and zero incidents are possible, one task at a time, minute by minute, day by day, that they could change the behavior of their entire workforce. They have demonstrated that beliefs can be altered and that through their training, daily messaging, hiring practices, recognition protocols, and foundational systems, they can be sustained. Most of all, they have demonstrated safety outcomes far superior to any other provider in their space. That is the power of positivity.

Alignment Makes People Believe

Many leaders believe that they can communicate their way out of a challenging situation. This was true for a leading children's hospital. The long-tenured leader was convinced that their payer-mix issues and philanthropic declines could be overcome through a new positioning and aggressive advertising campaign. He also believed he could cure the low morale of the physician group that drove the profitability of the health system. We conducted extensive research that included studying psychographic profiles, lifestyle, as well as attitudinal perspectives of its patient database for the previous five years, and the organizational identity inside the system. The data was shocking in the level of misalignment that existed. The disconnect was clear—what the system said they were all about was not accepted by the physicians, nurses, or patients. Each had high perceptions and regard for the system, but each came at it from a different mindset. Norming the mindsets and aligning all constituents around a cohesive strategy was paramount to the organization achieving its desired financial outcomes and preferred future state as a regional force.

The system took the research and ensuing strategy work to heart—creating as bold and aggressive a vision imaginable for a children's hospital—one that would ensure care for every child in the community. Most interesting with this vision, the board did not desire to compete in the national "beauty contests" and try to become one of the top two or three children's hospitals in the country. Rather, their vision was about impacting care and affecting meaningful change in access across every community they served.

With this bold vision adopted, they were then able to communicate a more authentic and compelling narrative. They developed a position around a fundamentally differentiated level of care. Everything about it was unique. They went to unusual efforts, over a week-long period, to get the entirety of the system, more than 4,000 employees and physicians, aligned and engaged. Each day for the rollout week, the leadership treated their employees with a differentiated level of attention, focus, and care to demonstrate their belief in the position, and even more so, their commitment to supporting employees in their delivery of it. The first day, leaders, including every member of the C-suite, were positioned at the entrance of garages welcoming employees as others were serving coffee and providing doughnuts as they entered. The next day, a pill bottle filled with jelly beans was distributed to every employee—noting that they were the prescription for successful patient outcomes. In the ensuing days, activities and support were provided to employees in a unique way that was consistent with the organizational vision. On the last day of the week, the leadership held hour-long presentations every other hour for 24 hours—explaining the vision and new position. Every employee was provided collateral, clothing with the logo, and creative, thought-provoking learning maps to reinforce the position. After each presentation, a beautifully catered "thanksgiving" meal (even though the event date was late spring) was served in the hospital courtyard with the message of thanks for being part of the health system.

The message of thanks combined with the aligned internal and external efforts transformed the health system's patient and financial outcomes. And, the expected happened—donors engaged to give to greatness. Alignment creates energy that others want to share in. People want to belong to a dream, plan, or initiative that is bigger than their individual experience. In clarity, we can see where the connections need to be made and design for them accordingly. There was a palpable energy and connectivity across every department and not only did they achieve their financial and philanthropic goals, their patient scores improved as well.

Alignment Supercharges Creativity

In Chapter 4, we explored how design and creativity is a foundational part of our consulting work. It supports the heavy-duty strategy and cultural work by creating a mood and helping with the understanding and acceptance of the change initiatives. It is not an outlier or add-on to what we do. It is embedded in every part of our organization and fundamental to our and our client's success.

One of our clients—a start-up that had increased the number of its employees by more than a thousand people in its first year—took a very purposeful, proactive approach to creating a fully aligned organization with natural energetic pathways to support work being conducted across the United States. Their intentionality was clear from the first day of operations, when they went through strategic and culture-defining exercises even though at that time the organization consisted of only three passionate professionals. It was their intention to create the expectations and encourage alignment with each future acquisition and hire.

On its one-year anniversary, in an attempt to take all the words—the vision, the values, the behaviors—they had put together to define the company and bring it to life, the leaders rolled out a boots-on-the-ground tour. They gathered people in town hall formats and reiterated what made their company so different. The words were powerful and inspiring. But, more so, it was the leader standing out in the open, with no notes, simply being himself and telling the story of where they were going together. He was genuine in his delivery, and perfect with his words, authenticity, and appeal. People were inspired and they believed.

At the end of the presentation, the leader said, "They don't call this the boots-on-the-ground tour for nothing"—before he pointed to the corner of the room, which was stacked with boxes of new branded boots for every employee. He said, "If we don't do the right thing from the ground up, we will never be successful," and then reiterated that the foundation of the values and behaviors was unshakable and defining. The creativity of the delivery and the positivity that his words and actions injected were lasting and meaningful. It was also measurable, as their results hit every goal they set. Most important, they established that they cared about one thing—doing things the right way for the employees.

Aligning with Good Is Great

There are times when employees feel disconnected with the business objectives of the organization or with the dispersed footprint of the organization. On a lower level, they are aligned with the values and the people, but on a higher level, for whatever reason, they don't fully understand the strategy or direction the company is going in. They do their job within the bounds that are set. In these organizations, often large and sometimes impersonal, the alignment of the workforce can come through efforts outside the traditional work environment. In these companies, we have helped create cause-related initiatives that are as much about doing good in the community as giving the workforce something to rally around, embody, and feel good about.

Throughout my career, the social or cause marketing element has been foundational for many of our clients around the country. For a client's hundredth anniversary, the celebration theme centered around "our roots run deep." Coming off a historic drought in the region, the cause campaign focused on bringing the roots theme to life in the workforce, so we recommended that the company donate a huge number of trees in each employee's honor and give the employee time off to be part of the planting and community rejuvenation efforts. To support the theme and build internal pride, we posted the "our roots run deep" theme on a billboard, which was made to look like a tree, including the pole wrapped in vinyl to represent bark. The message inside and outside the organization was shared, and more importantly, good was delivered as well.

In our own company, every employee is given their own foundation, with an annual $1,000 grant. The fund, which is titled with the employees' names followed by Deutser Clarity Fund, is the employee's to give away to not-for-profit organizations of their choosing. This is our way to align the company on the importance of giving back and give employees a feel-good way to lead that effort. Many corporations have established matching grants and offer a paid day each year when an employee can volunteer for a favorite cause.

We encourage leaders to align and connect these efforts through clarity. Include good works in your values and vision if that is to be part of your organization. Tap the people dimension in your box to innovate ways for employees to become involved and fully engaged. We've seen many companies offer these opportunities, but without alignment throughout the organization, they can become mere mentions in an orientation packet. Breathe some life into these efforts. Doing good for others creates connections and positive energy.

Alignment with Values Has Value

We have long learned that just because someone has a title of authority doesn't mean that they are a leader. There are characteristics that are core to a true leader. We have been fortunate to work with wonderful leaders, men and women of extraordinary character who are committed to doing right, even when the circumstances can dictate or direct otherwise.

One of our former clients came to us with a request for help with his new position. We were stunned because we were the reason he was in the new position, at a new company, in a new city, in the first place. Our firm had been brought into his former company to do a study with the CEO's intent to replace this person with someone else. Only after we began our work did we realize that we were being set up and his impending firing was a done deal—regardless of our findings. Instead of giving in, we dug in deeper to make sure the study was done with integrity, respect, and dignity. Our findings were consistent with the CEO's original beliefs, and we made the difficult recommendation to replace the leader.

So, several months later when he called us for help, we were surprised and asked him, "Why would you call us, knowing we did that to you?" He responded, "I'll never forget what you did to and for me—you treated me with dignity and respect and I will forever remember your professionalism in an environment that didn't value it. Your values prevailed and for that, I am grateful." Amazingly, he gave us the chance to work with him to transform his new company and became one of our largest clients. More important than the relationship (and friendship) we developed was his continued demonstration of doing right and his lasting lessons on what it meant to be a true professional and a gentleman. This example is a constant reminder to our team of the important life lesson: Do what is right and it will come back to you.

The most successful companies have a fully aligned workforce and an undeniable, positive energy that permeates the organization. And from them, we have seen that what matters most about alignment is that it changes the flow of things. You begin to see that your efforts are both bringing intended results as well as attracting other positives, resources, and assets you hadn't imagined. It creates an ease within the effort, not one that suggests you sit back, but rather one that propels you forward because you can feel the surge of energy that surrounds your efforts and even your solutions. We have a core value at Deutser that encapsulates what alignment brings.

We Love What We Do and It Shows

CHAPTER 7

Masqueraders of Clarity

W e've explored how circuit breakers can affect the flow of energy throughout an organization, affecting alignment, and impeding impact. For the most part, circuit breakers are created from within our own history, insecurities, faults, and bad habits. Over the past several decades, I have come to recognize that there is another category of energy wasters that we engage with that masquerade as something or someone who will bring value and forward motion, but in reality, are tricksters. In their best light, they waste your time. In the revealing light of clarity, they can be found to cloud thinking and often put teams and organizations on an imposter's path that leads to somewhere else, taking them away from their core and creating the fractured energy of something that is not what it seems. The waste of time, energy, and money that is invested and often exhausted on these masqueraders can be significant. I want here to expose a few masqueraders of clarity that we've encountered in our work. Understanding and being able to recognize these masqueraders is fundamental to operating and leading in clarity.

POLITICAL CORRECTNESS

There is a tug from the world that encourages the average and reveals only 50 percent of the truth. This is political correctness at its core and it is one of the great masqueraders. We have allowed society to dictate that political correctness is the clear and comfortable way. It has become our standard time and time again. We've all been led in this dance and carefully taught the steps of acceptable behavior and tolerant language. But this great masquerader is not truthful and it defers the social and societal conversation to be completed at a later date, or worse, allows the real issues to simmer uncontested for long periods.

Political correctness holds judgment by the very term "correctness" letting us know that there is an acceptable right way to think and act. It replaces our words and beliefs with those that belong to others and were set as standards by people who may hold different values from ours. We have been made to believe that it neutralizes offensive thoughts, words, and behaviors, but it really just dresses the people up like an unruly child made to wear a tight-fitting suit, until he tears it off and shows his true nature. We have lost honesty at the expense of judgment and conformity. Political correctness within an organization can, and usually will, lead to a negative impact somehow or somewhere. A perceptive 2013 article by Howard S. Schwartz expresses the deep-rooted implications political correctness may have, explaining how "Political correctness may be considered to represent control over discourse. If that were all it were, it would be a matter of little concern to organizations. However, organizational decisions involve positions that are proposed and defended through discourse. Hence political correctness must imply control over organizational decision-making, and hence over every aspect of the organization. The implication of this is that the psychological dynamics that underlie political correctness come to be the underlying dynamics of the organization as a whole." Political correctness is often two sides saying what neither wants to say, which makes it impossible to get to the truth because you are dealing with only part of the information.

Political correctness makes it clear that there is a line that can't be crossed, but like a bad surveyor, you often miscalculate where the line is, so you back off or shut down or dance around like a fool without either side knowing what really needs to be addressed. Instead, you say or do something that has been deemed acceptable and safe. This makes it virtually impossible to have clarity because this clever masquerader would have us believe that being acceptable and safe is the same thing as giving respect. The sad truth of political correctness is that while it masquerades as respect, it is only a watered-down conversation that leads to increased confusion accompanied by an undercurrent of resentment and ill will. We miss the opportunity to have open discourse and debate about what really matters because much of what we want to say has been labeled as too offensive, risky, or inflammatory. There is a great yearning for an eventual necessary balance that must be addressed as the pendulum swings to find a more authentic equilibrium in our society and in the world in which we live and work. Instead of creating a false sense of inclusion, in clarity, you can make an actual return to value.

When leaders make critical decisions based on politically correct information, they are making educated guesses—which 50 percent is true or applicable versus evaluating the situation for what it is with a 100 percent of the information. Yes, there must be a sensitivity lens applied, but the lens that is needed is simply a lens to help soften the perspective, not fundamentally redefine it. Our society has dictated that being safe is more important than telling the full truth, and our leaders are wary to cross, or in many cases, even get close to that line. They deem the risk too great, even when the risk is less scary than making decisions based on incomplete or skewed information. In some of the world's largest companies, we have seen political correctness derail critical projects because leaders across the world, in an effort to eliminate any potential for offending someone, were unwilling to have the real conversation until it was too late.

The negative impact of political correctness was on full display at a global energy company that invested millions of dollars in transformational technology over a several-years period to streamline, and in many ways reinvent, the organization's global communication and engagement function. In effect, their goal was to fundamentally change the way work gets done across the international giant. The translation, regardless of which country in which they operated, communicated that the way they used to work was going to change and people were going to be forced to do things differently. People began to retreat to their comfort zones and in small like-minded groups mourn the changes, which were designed to drive progress. The company had developed the system of the future, but because of the cultural sensitivities that exist across borders, the unwillingness to ruffle feathers, and the desire for political correctness, no one was willing to say what either wanted to say, which was the system would not work in today's environment and they would each work to kill it when it was implemented. The massive global structure of the organization allowed and even encouraged this behavior, and because the project cost remained in the single-digit millions, it would be a rounding error when it was killed. The problem was not with this rounding error, but with the hundreds of other projects that were killed because of shallow, politically correct conversation. The shareholders deserved a better outcome. So, too, do the workers on the frontlines who benefit most by the technological advancements that the managers far above them killed with political correctness.

In other situations, clients have come to us with veiled innuendos and words about politics, religion, or other taboo subjects. Most companies shy away from the conversation while we work to construct clarity, which must include confronting an issue head on, regardless of the politically correct point of view. This can ensure absolute transparency for all involved on defining who we each are, what we believe, and how we lead. It is uncomfortable for some, but it has saved us from participating in projects with people we don't share the same values with or the same perspective. Organizations have struggled to have meaningful conversations around issues because one or more leaders may be perceived as insensitive or out of step. There is such great fear, even in a boardroom or executive suite, that one outlying perspective might actually destroy a colleague's career over what one might perceive as an inappropriate comment, out of the mainstream, or not politically correct. The question remains: Who defines the mainstream? All too often, it is left undebated out of fear to have an honest, relevant, and necessary conversation. When a leader puts a stake in the ground, he or she is vulnerable to attack from the other polarized and often politicized side. Unfortunately, there are too many people who masquerade as leaders, but who are really spineless cowards who would rather sit silently and twist a person's words or worse, mischaracterize their intent to damage their reputation in the name of political correctness.

A common experience that we encounter involves the inevitable conversation on the company handbook or policy manual and whether to identify employees as "he" and "she" or "they" or some other pronoun. When the discussion turns to how to identify individuals with pronouns or whether to have a gender or sexual orientation policy at all, conversation is immediately stifled in the room out of fear. You can feel the energy in the room change as people who are normally outspoken and honest clam up, and others gently try to deflect or redirect the conversation. People then leave the meeting and have conversations in their safe zones with like-minded people, only hardening their stance and furthering the solution for the company. Again, some groups believe that by bringing up the sensitive subject, they have achieved success. Yet, in clarity, we recognize that simply delays the inevitable conversation, or worse, leaves the organization open and unprepared when a problem arises. Our solution is to ensure an open, honest, and transparent conversation with both sides, or extremes, discussed. By refusing to allow the half-conversation in the middle and forcing the full, albeit sometimes uncomfortable conversation, the group has pierced the tension and encouraged more healthy behavior. There are many examples across virtually every type and size company of how political correctness has derailed the honest conversation and directed them down the wrong path. We have seen organizations for whom the conversation is stymied simply because of the sensitivity of the subject matter. Living the old adage that it is better to not let someone know what are your political or religious beliefs may lessen conflict, but it does not necessarily lead to open, productive, or healthy conversations. How many times do we hear the comment that "he voted for XYZ candidate, who is an idiot"; therefore, he believes the same things and brings the same biases as that candidate. Simply going out of our way to recognize the other side and the fact that there may be areas of commonality, even in a polarized world, we are able to bridge conversations and increase respect. This allows a conversation—not necessarily agreement—that at the very least provides clarity, without the vitriol, of where each person or group stands. More issues were avoided by simply sharing where they were standing in the first place and not allowing political correctness to derail them and undo any shared foundation of understanding. The masquerade is not moving organizations forward; it is holding them back and deferring critical issues heading for a future, and often vicious, never-ending fight.

SUCK-UPS AND PEOPLE PLEASERS

Why has this time-tested reroute held up for generations? Because people like validation and the ego can masquerade as alignment, especially when someone is actually building on a false foundation. This behavior requires enormous energy and tending, and can quickly prompt the question in clarity, why not put all that same energy into the work and be excellent instead of merely appearing to be excellent? Suck-ups are *yes* people and as such, oppose clarity. When generous, they are telling you 50 percent of the truth and withholding the other 50 percent to serve their own purpose and to use strategically when it will best enhance their position.

Suck-ups and people pleasers are everywhere in every business. They masquerade as leaders, often found on the ladder to top positions or as a staff member whom the leader relies heavily on and, as such, has the leader's ear, attention, and time. They are people, who by title, tenure, or position, are poised to champion, protect, move forward, or hold back a project, initiative, or cause depending on the personal benefit that they can derive. Where the masquerade begins is when their own ambition or self-protectionism taints the flow of data and information up the chain of leadership. They lay their path with words and evidence that supports what they believe the leader most wants to hear or confirms a key concept that the leader is promoting. They are often manipulating information and data—and always manipulating access. Suck-ups and people pleasers often thrive in smaller and even family-owned companies. Even when the next generation is brought in, they often surround themselves with people who will please their parent/founder. Suck-ups also flourish when leaders make bad decisions. These masqueraders add energy and validation to a bad decision. They often don't have the skillset to navigate difficult circumstances or crucial conversations, so they ride along with the unsuspecting or faulty leader as far as it will take them.

We see these examples everywhere in business today as people try to survive in their place of work, worrying less about the quality of the work product they deliver and more about the longevity of their tenure. Years ago, we recognized that the second-in-command at a large retail chain was adept at serving as a buffer between the leader and the team, never giving either enough details to have clarity and working the missing pieces to his advantage. He would pose issues and then magically make them appear to go away. In reality, this individual was a poser who was simply playing up to the egocentric CEO. He was allowing scenarios to develop and exacerbate them in order to be the hero with the solution, making himself indispensable through a situation that never needed to exist. The sad reality was that the narcissistic leader used the people pleaser to feed his own ego. They fed each other what they needed. It was almost like a scene from *The Little Shop of Horrors*, with each saying to the other, "Feed me," or in other words, feed my ego. Unfortunately, outside of their circle, no one in the organization benefited by the unhealthy dance.

In another organization, a 19-year employee, "a company survivor," had earned her reputation as one who could outlast any leader or any change. She was adept at navigating between leaders at every level of the organization. She brought value through historical perspective and understanding on seemingly critical components of operation. Her smile and outward personality were contagious. But below the surface of service and devotion and happy facade she was a master at sucking up at the right time to the right person to ensure her voice was heard and to show her support and "concern" for anything that the leadership might not readily understand or immediately approve of. In other words, she had a knack for poisoning the water by floating her concerns, even long before the potential solution was ready for presentation. As a mid-level employee, she had the ability to negatively change the direction of any initiative with her behind-the-scenes manuervering, manipulations, and people-pleasing. She was often the voice of the CEO when he wasn't available. She worked in a stealthy fashion using her "people equity" that she had gathered over years of people-pleasing to place her agenda at the forefront by making incremental moves that most were not able to detect, when she was always so helpful and always had the "greater good" as her intention. Then, with her patented line, she would respond, "Yes, sir," to every request the CEO made while quietly leaking her toxic touch on the status of all that she did not herself favor. That phrase has become as dangerous a combination as we have seen, especially when it is delivered by people-pleasers and suck-ups. The "yes, sir" masks the true intention or meaning. It is simply a gratuitous blow-off line, seemingly delivered with respect.

Suck-ups and people-pleasers are often found with one of two compelling personal agendas: an eye toward promotion or devotion to personal security established through longevity in the organization. Their masquerade is effective because they seem genuinely concerned, are usually well-liked because they tell people what they want to hear, and make themselves indispensable through actions that often involve manipulation of information, people, or both. Within an organization, they can also be feared for their tactics and close relation with key decision makers. We fall for these masqueraders because we are attracted to their devotion, team spirit, and because they generally make us feel good. But, in clarity, we see that they are not aligned because of the distortions and half-truths created and fueled by their own needs. They are certainly liked and often depended upon. Each of these masqueraders eventually reminds the leader of a company or a department that we are all only as good as the people around us because, in clarity, we recognize that we are all connected, and without purposeful attention, we drift toward the lowest common denominator.

PAST PERFORMANCE

History, while it can be an indicator, does not dictate or ensure future performance. Yet, all too often, organizations are stymied by the constant reliance on the past, for example, "This always works"; "Why change what's working?"; "I've always done it this way."

Variables in our business environment are constantly evolving and changing. The chaos that we are tasked with navigating is undeterred by the solutions that once worked in a far simpler, slower moving world. Even one variance can greatly skew results and outcomes. The answer is, as a well-known CEO once said, "Every great strategy will eventually fail." The reliance on and connection to the past disallows our energy to be in the present or to morph into a necessary future state. It makes us derivative instead of original, meek instead of bold, and can trick us to be like the frog in a pot of boiling water that doesn't notice that the temperature is rising. Okay, no animals were harmed in the making of this theory, but you get my point.

Since we are constantly experiencing change, past performance could be more suitably viewed as a retrospective, much like that of an artist, which shows as we take in the artifacts that serve as witness to the genesis of an idea that grows and becomes something of a masterpiece rather than holding on to or repurposing something that once worked, even gloriously, but never evolved to accommodate changes and advancements.

This tired masquerader keeps us steeped in past glory where we might experience admiration and acknowledgment, as this trickster robs us of the full expression of our ever-evolving abilities and potential. Stuck in the past, we can never be fully realized. When stuck, we are unable to unleash our truest and most present powers. Clarity demands that we make ourselves fully available for mastery.

Best Practices and Outdated Mandates

Many leaders place their focus on best practices and industry-leading practices. Instead of being stuck in our own past performance, here we are adopting the energy of what someone else made work in an entirely different organizational culture, with different components, talents, and resources. This masquerades as a good idea because if it has worked for others—after all, why expend your own time and resources for something original when outcomes may be more reliable if following someone else's tried-and-true path?

Giving attention to an adopted best practice can be helpful while learning or developing because it provides a shortcut and can help make you operational more quickly, but once you have your own competency, cut it loose and work toward what might be a better fit for your own organization. Through all our work, we understand that practices for one leading organization don't necessarily transfer as successfully to another organization. Yet, too often, those practices are adopted or forced into the new organization, masking themselves as clarity. Many times this happens because it worked for the leader before in a past life or because it provides cover in the event it doesn't work—the leader has the easy out: We adopted the same best practices as.... While it can be safer and is often easier to adopt what others have done, it works against everything we believe and do for our clients.

This masquerader also destroys a company's ability to innovate and leaves value on the table. For every efficiency gain that can come from adopting a best practice, there is a lost opportunity for an organization to find an even better way to do something, or find a value driver for one of their customers. When we assume that a practice is already at its best, we are accepting that no more innovation is possible. Every client is unique, and so, too, are the solutions that drive them. This doesn't preclude them from adopting the best practices; it simply becomes one of several options. Then the nuance matters. Practices often include hiring, inventory and supply management, organizational redundancies, and so many others. In clarity, practices that are best for others usually won't fit in your box once it is constructed and properly built out. While it can serve as a temporary structure, something of your own making becomes a more organic fit. Don't let this jack-in-the box masquerader pop up because it masquerades as a fit for your developing culture and organization.

Similar to the adoption of best practices from others, leftovers that once worked well in your own organization can last for years without anyone challenging them or putting any energy into reexamining or replacing them. This is often contested when there is a change of leadership, acquisition, new ownership, or merger, but the best time to address inherited mandates is before the stress of change makes it necessary. The state of being in clarity requires this masquerader to perpetually shift throughout the process to stay current and relevant in a changing landscape. Don't push something forward just because it is the way it has always been done. Take the initiative, instead, to check the alignment to see if it still fits.

Sadly, we see this masquerader in action in companies that are failing, or worse, that have ceased operations after years of "doing things the way we have always done them." Years ago,

I worked for the famed Ringling Bros. and Barnum & Bailey Circus. Like all promoters, I had a binder that spelled out the specifics of how everything was done, passed down from decade to decade, and rarely questioned. This became the bible that we all lived by and worked from regardless of the city, the environment, or the show (there were multiple circuses, and we also promoted Walt Disney World on Ice, as well). When you deviated from the mandate defined in the typeset, xeroxed binder, you invariably received a call from corporate headquarters, or worse, from a colleague promoting a show in another market chastising you for deviating from a mandate that has always worked, and that "we all live by." It didn't matter that the innovation I introduced at the circus or ice show (in one instance it was the promotion of a hockey exhibition game between the Disney characters from the cast and the local city's professional hockey team, which was held during intermission, and was wildly entertaining and more aggressive than we could have ever expected) drove attendance, interest, and positively shifted the narrative in the media community. The audience loved it, but my colleagues chastised me for breaking from the best practices they used every day.

With Ringling Bros., you would think it was the romance of the deep tradition that resulted in so little change, and while that was part of it, it was more that they were missing the fact that the world was changing, especially in regard to entertainment, technology, and especially animal rights. Tradition and outdated mandates are often found as terrible twins in organizations.

POLICY

Policy is often code for "this is what we least like to deal with, so here's our policy on it." Plain and simple, policies exist as a perceived protection—for a company, its employees, or an individual. Predictably, they serve as basic, average rules instead of commonsense guidelines. They are engineered to strip people from making individual decisions, thereby providing perceived protection for the employer. Policies force employees to hide behind a series of words that in actuality removes power and authority from them. Simply do as the words say and you will be a valued member of the tribe, provided, of course, that you are on the right side of the policy. But what policies often communicate to employees is that they are not trusted, and even though qualified and appropriately trained, they are not to use their own judgment to make decisions. They are instead to follow policy. Policies can be effective if designed to include employee discernment, the application of common sense, and a structure for swift escalation to resolution if the employee needs additional help or consultation. But most often, policies are a masquerade, starting with their creation when they are designed to provide answers for broad application. This is further perpetuated through adoption and execution, thought to be efficient by repeatable actions and mindless answers without the need for knowing the details of a situation since the answer will be the same regardless. Clarity allows space and structure for something other than a narrowly prescribed code of behavior, and encourages openness and dialogue when there is a difference of opinion or insight into guidelines.

An overuse of internal policies is a poor substitute for good management. For example, an oldie but goodie is an infractions policy that is typically put in place to put employees on notice as to what they are *not* supposed to do. Employers will hold you accountable for tiny infractions and keep track of them in a report or "file." Employees are at work—not in prison. Managers are forced to become policy guards who are more focused on what employees are doing wrong than right. How many of these policies encourage positive notes placed in the employee file?

Could you imagine if the same minute details are recorded on both ends—good and poor performance—of the behavioral spectrum? The point is that the policy often encourages the collection of negative data rather than a balance of the two, which would require incessant collection and aggregation of information. As it is employed in most companies, this is an employee engagement killer.

Outside of our own workplaces, we see other examples in our personal lives as well. Have you ever been on the phone with an employee from the airlines with any of a host of issues (fill in the blank from any of your own personal experiences) who can only cite, "I'm sorry, sir, but that is our policy." The retort is always the same, "I understand the policy, but this situation, not of my own making, requires special consideration and a smidge of common sense." The conversation returns, "That is our policy. I'm sorry," (the phrase that could become a masquerader because they are neither feeling compassion nor sorrow in any way—they are doing what they have been taught, to rigidly cling to policy when in doubt). The now 30-minute back-and-forth (it is not really a conversation) has cost the airline and the customer as well as the employee's effectiveness in representing the company.

There are entire industries built on policy masquerading as clarity—as seen in the insurance business. Whether it is health or home insurance, the insured know that they are paying for a policy to protect them. Unfortunately, most of us are unaware of what the policy even covers, and we are ill equipped as lay people against the cascade of legal maneuvering and fine print that often guts much of what we think we are protected against. The homeowner, who is required to have insurance, has a false sense of security and learns only long after the fact that they are not covered because of a heretofore unknown exclusion. Health insurance policies cater to the needs and the economic benefit of the insurance company and health industry. Individuals depend on politicians to help through regulation and standards, yet they are often part of the problem by not doing what is right for individuals, only what is politically expedient. If they widened their view to include more clarity on the issues that face and protect the individual, policies would read very differently, with language and organization that easily and in clear words discloses vulnerabilities.

Policy also clouds clarity for organizations, often in the governmental space, as part of winning contract bids, which often requires the inclusion of a minority, female-owned, small business, or disadvantaged business, regardless of the acumen of the business or the sophistication of their solution. This policy, like a quota, masquerades as a fair process to ensure equality, although the purchaser (in most cases an agent of the taxpaying public) is either paying up to one third more for the work (or the winning bidder has already marked up his or her bid), or worse, the hiring organization is getting a potentially inferior and definitely less integrated product deliverable. The intent is to provide an opportunity for those who would otherwise not be considered for the work. In actuality, it provides a disadvantage to the end user, who should be focused on the highest quality deliverable at the most fair price. When the most-qualified companies choose not to participate in the process or solicit the work because of a policy that directs the money they rightfully earn to others for no other reason than the size of their business or their gender or race, it demeans the quality and effectiveness of their work and becomes a masquerader.

We are all faced with policies masquerading as clarity on a daily basis—think no further than the service industry and the lack of control the employee has to do what is right and the inability of the customer to get what he or she needs and deserves. There are companies that have policies that are not masqueraders—companies whose policies empower the worker to make the right decision. But, most often, company policies end up serving as masqueraders that provide cover or permission for employees or companies to not do the right thing. The most revered companies aren't looking for policy to define behavior and dictate outcomes. Rather, they seek clarity in finding

MASQUERADERS UNMASKED

MASQUERADER TYPES

Best Practices + Outdated Mandates (p. 205)   Past Performance (p. 204)

Boards + Founders (p. 214)   Policy (p. 207)

Cause (p. 217)   Political Correctness (p. 195)

Compliance (p. 213)   Politics (p. 218)

Leaders + Managers (p. 220)   Suck-ups + People Pleasers (p. 201)

Figure 7.1   Masqueraders Unmasked

List up to five masqueraders found in your company.

1. _____
2. _____
3. _____
4. _____
5. _____

How do your masqueraders negatively impact your company?

_____
_____
_____
_____

What steps can be taken to "unmask" (remove) your masqueraders?

1. _____
2. _____
3. _____
4. _____
5. _____

How would this positively impact your company?

_____
_____
_____
_____

solutions, often based in common sense, higher levels of training, and an appropriate delegation of authority that empower people on the frontlines to act within a set of standards to "do the right thing for the customer." These companies accept that sometimes the solution may be costlier than what a prescribed, generic solution may be, but the win of an empowered "now, not mindless" employee and satisfied customer way outweigh, in both the short and the long term, the relatively minor additional costs incurred by the decision outside the prescribed policy. In clarity, everyone eventually wins. And when the person making the policy is clear on the impact on not one but all constituents, then the policy can be crafted to create the necessary outcome.

COMPLIANCE

This clarity masquerader is all about doing the least required. It often involves a checklist of things one is required to do and, once done, everything will supposedly be fine. Compliance is often mistaken for clear direction. Compliance alone doesn't work to engage your full understanding, talent, and intelligence. Simply checking a box doesn't mean that you're truly committed. It devalues each of us to the lowest common denominator.

Compliance, which is a necessary and required evil in many industries, has become the safety hook that many leaders and organizations latch onto for protection. It is often linked to governmental or industry regulation, and increasingly companies are focused on simply meeting the compliance standards. Piling on policies and regulations has seemingly made it a burden to even comply. Achieving these minimum standards creates a disconnect for companies that aspire to greatness.

Some of the greatest safety-related tragedies in our country were caused by highly compliant companies, with employees who did their job and checked the boxes. In compliant companies, common sense is replaced with the compliant focus and mindset—do only what I have to get done. Compliant workers are not ill-intending or incompetent; rather, they are following the direction of their company's leaders who require and often evaluate and reward based on it.

Professionals do what they are expected to do, creating an illusion of safety or high performance when it is only the minimum standards being met. They sometimes interpret that any change or reach beyond what is communicated is taking them outside of safety, and as such, creating vulnerabilities with unknown consequences. As we have discussed in earlier chapters, compliance and commitment are closely related as different sides of the same coin. Some companies create programs or initiatives that masquerade as commitment, when in actuality, they are simply checking the box of compliance for a customer or prospective customer as a standard that they desire or to "live up to" a governmental standard.

Our masquerader also calls out the need to make a distinction between demonstrating and complying. Demonstrating is taking an intention and value outward, putting it into action, and embracing it. Complying is doing it because it is a requirement or because you feel you have to in order to "be safe" or "be accountable." The obligatory appearance is well known throughout industries. True alignment means that you are part of something larger happening and you "show up" because you're a part of it!

BOARDS AND FOUNDERS

Boards bring a different level of complexity to the masquerader topic. Boards have a specific function within organizations—almost unanimously created to provide the highest-level strategic direction and fiscal oversight. The other most-visible and critical function is the hiring and firing of the CEO. Overwhelmingly, board members understand and fulfill this responsibility. Where clarity comes into play is when the boundaries around the board become blurred or compromised. Where does strategy stop and operations start? Boards become masqueraders when they begin to knowingly or unknowingly assume the responsibilities of the CEO and leadership team or when they insert their personal or professional expertise or directive into the equation at the expense of the leaders and even the organization. By their nature, board members are selected for their business acumen, fiscal prowess, or standing in an industry or community. In other words, they have been successful in their business or line of work and bring a measure of performance to the equation (again, note past performance). They are also leaders who bring a strong point of view and have no issue sharing that perspective.

In not-for-profit organizations, people often get recruited for boards because they offer a particular expertise, important industry or community connection, or philanthropic capability, but frequently don't have the breadth of business-specific or industry understanding to solve the complex, multidimensional problems at hand. They have skills, money, a voice, and influence, and while that initially masquerades as meeting the organization's needs, it often clouds clarity as complex issues arise. In the end, the board member exerts his or her influence, yet the organization's executive is still left accountable—even when the solution set is dictated, or worse, demanded. The leader cannot push back on his or her bosses when they intervene on a regular basis—nor can the leader survive in the long term without pushing back, which creates an interesting conundrum. As the line continues to get blurred, it becomes clearer that some board members too often get involved to fulfill needs of their own self-interest, such as building a resume, pushing the organization to hire a friend or close business associate as a vendor, or as a prequel to running for public office, which can lead to highly dysfunctional power plays.

There are times that even well-intending boardmembers make decisions that on the surface seem to be furthering the business objectives of the organization, but in reality are a masquerader for operational control or furthering an individual's powerbase. A powerful board chair appointed a rogue, outspoken, and agenda-driven board member to lead an influential committee. The intent was to reward the board member for her service because of her loyalty (which is not the same as integrity) to the chair, and supposedly, the institution. It became clear, however, that the board chair was intent on wielding a strong hand in the oversight and direction of the marketing and outreach of the business under the guise of "the board's strategic responsibilities." This was an obvious conflict with the board's stated responsibilities and far outside their professional skillset. The highly skilled marketing team was relegated to not being smart and strategic, but political—gutting their will and the quality of their work. Boards can also be "pay for play," which means that they are doubling as critical contributors (not simply financial) and as such, are rewarded with a seat or higher position on the board. Power and self-interest go hand in hand, which can make for an intoxicating cocktail for this masquerader.

While boards are, on the whole, good and productive, there are invariably members who must be unmasked for the good of the institution and the integrity of the board. It takes only one board member to cast a shadow on the whole of the board. The redirected board member now brings industry experience as a foundation to understanding the business, not directing it; reorients his perspective to ensure that his constituency group is not best served, but the whole of the institution; is a vocal advocate for the strategic direction, but is committed to supporting, and holding accountable, the professional leader for implementing and bringing it to life.

While a board's power and responsibilities can vary from company to company and industry to industry, we find they are most effective in a governance role, for setting the organization's vision, for reviewing the CEO's performance (hiring and firing), and for working with and supporting the CEO in achieving the stated strategic objectives for the business. Anything beyond that is an overreach, especially as it relates to strategy. In clarity, a board's responsibilities must be clearly stated, strategically led, and continually revisited.

CAUSE

Most people don't think about doing good in the community as a masquerader—after all, people or causes are positively affected. I agree. But, there are many instances where leaders, corporations, or businesses use their good, concerned public face to masquerade bad business behavior.

We have worked in a city in which a leader is hailed as a humble, caring hero. He is somehow always front-and-center when tragedy strikes, ready with a noble gesture. But what the community doesn't see is that he has a crafty cover. His demand for media attention for every perceived "good" deed pulls the focus away from poor business practices and the questionable strategies he employs. So externally, he masquerades as a hero, but those who work for him see the truer, darker side. No one would dare speak out about the ulterior motivations for fear of retribution by the leader and his suck-ups or the rebukes by the community that he has so carefully duped.

Of course, no one can speak to the true motivations of another, but when "good" causes are used as a strategy to bump "good" business, such subterfuges can create a gap in clarity. This contrasts with leaders who quietly do right and good by the community because it is the right thing to do. They do not seek publicity; it finds them, often when they are not expecting it. They are clear that their purpose rests solely on their contributions.

We have seen this masquerader in full effect when a wildly successful energy company continually forced the philanthropic issue in the community where their headquarters were located, making wild grants and challenging leaders of other large companies to match them. Their philanthropy and do-gooder spirit created an undeniable energy, and a competitive spirit that fueled giving and elevated causes important to them. Unfortunately for the causes most important to them, their business practices were ultimately unmasked and the good deeds were seen for what they were not. They masked their self-serving bad behavior for a long time because of the reputation they built and the perceived generosity that drove help to others.

Giving back to the community that supports and makes you successful is a fundamental principle to our firm. It is a requirement in order to become a client. Cause or socially responsible marketing is a powerful tool, but one that quickly exposes the inner core of the company—those who are committed for the right reasons always succeed, and those who do good for some other, nefarious, reason always end up getting unmasked because it is not true to their DNA.

Politics

While you have read earlier that politics is intricately interwoven in many of the other masqueraders, I wanted to also call it out on its own because by its very nature, politics is one of the great and most destructive masqueraders. Whether it is on the national landscape or in a small family office, politics are part of our daily and professional lives and masquerade in many different ways.

Politics are rarely, if ever, about doing what is right for the whole of a company or organization. Politics is about serving someone's or something's best self-interest. It is often linked with political correctness and rarely incorporates anywhere near 100 percent of the truth. So many leadership teams are rife with politics, which often impairs their ability to lead with clarity and certainty, instead of doing what is best for the whole of the organization. This permeates many elected positions and organizations that don't have strong, committed and accountable leadership.

Politics masquerades as leadership, but in fact, it is only survival of the weak-minded elected or appointed official. We see politics masquerading in school districts and colleges across the country, where elected leaders are more focused on the business of the school as opposed to the education of the students. They design a structure intended to protect the politician and their cronies at the expense of those they are entrusted to protect. We also see this in organizations in which the CEO is caught between board members pushing for change and those holding on for the status quo, or worse, when CEOs acquiesce to a board's short-sighted directive against the long-term best interest, solely for survival.

So, whether you identify politics as its own masquerader or you see it as a function of another masquerader, this topic ensures that what you see on the surface is not often what you get. The clarity comes when the politics are pierced and doing right prevails, even when that means taking the ultimate professional risk and doing what is right over the objection of a senior leader demanding some other solution.

LEADERS AND MANAGERS

When describing leaders and managers, many organizations use the positions as interchangeable. Managers masquerading as leaders and leaders masquerading as managers create long-term issues inside organizations and often stunt the company's ability to perform. We hear frustrated senior leaders opining about how their managers struggle to lead important change initiatives, not accepting that their roles and skillsets are very different. The leaders may see the opportunity with a higher level of clarity, not often understanding or fully appreciating the manager's role in doing everything it takes to implement the necessary change. To the natural leader, they simply look at the situation and can't imagine everyone not being an immediate, willing follower. That is why we work so hard to unmask the differences of each critical function. When we work with clients on developing their unique behavioral competencies, assuming that the requisite knowledge, skills, and abilities for the position are met, we purposely define the expected behaviors for both managers and leaders, proving that one cannot masquerade as the other.

Of all the competency sorts that we have led with companies and organizations large and small, for-profit, and not-for-profit, private and public, not one, in hundreds and hundreds of sorts, has yielded the same result, with no two organizations being alike. Each company selected their own collection of competencies and then created their own unique definition and application. But the data, when aggregated, does yield some commonality. Over the past couple of decades, the more common behaviors our clients have identified as being key to creating clarity around leadership's and management's roles in driving organizational performance include:

Leadership Behaviors

Strategic thinking

Leading change

Inspiring others

Communicating effectively

Engaging customers

Managerial Behaviors

Setting expectations

Motivating direct reports

Developing talent

Organizing and planning work

Championing customer needs

In conclusion, masquerades are a system of diversion tactics, or better yet, *aversion tactics;*—survival mechanisms that are implemented out of fear: fear of failure, fear of conflict, fear of the difficult interactions that need to take place, fear of wrongfully accommodating all of the individual stakeholders of a group.

On the other end, as forms of diversion, they create a sidestep of a tense situation to temporarily alleviate the anxieties of those involved because of it. These diversions are like a forced smile, put on to cover up anguish on the face beneath, or the simple "I'm fine," when you know there is something wrong but you're not in a comfortable-enough environment in which that sharing and openness is promoted or actively received by others. Diversion to the past or relying on the past is a way of shortcutting the necessary actions and work that needs to take place for things to be done completely and wholesomely in their own right at this time. Past performances are a way of saying, "Well, look what I've done. What worked for me and what could work for us," as opposed to "Look what we should do. Look what we will do that can work for us now." You can take components from what you've learned in the past, but when you try to superimpose that past onto the present, you end up failing to account for all the areas of changed components that make up the now from when they used to be.

Altogether, these masqueraders have one thing in common: avoiding reality; avoiding the hard work that needs to be implemented in order to create the systems that one deserves; avoiding the gap between individuals' ideas or viewpoints; avoiding the pursuit of a common goal for the individual betterment of those involved; avoiding potentially discomforting conversations by mincing one's words and keeping oneself at a distance; or avoiding the repercussions of stating what's actually going on in one's mind by suppressing or limiting what one actually shares with the group or the public. Why have a real, down-to-earth conversation that may be uncomfortable when we can just sidestep it altogether by not voicing our opinions at all?

In short, these masqueraders are a form of survival mechanism that are used far too often, sometimes accidentally, and other times intentionally. But all the same, they end up degrading the interactions in the in-between and redirecting the outcome that best serves neither the organization nor the leader.

CHAPTER 8

Clarity as Process,
aka Magic

Throughout this book, we have helped you create and construct space within your organization where you can be in clarity. Everything we have built is applicable to organizations of all sizes, structures, and industries, as well as to the men and women who lead them. You now have both tools and an understanding of how clarity can bring value to your organization.

I want to propose one final component. It isn't one that can be plotted on a strategy map or that involves recruiting a star team member. Actually, it is more of a process than a single component, known as *alchemy*. In the traditional use of the word, alchemy is a biochemical process through which something is transformed. In clarity, this transformation occurs as the energy created by each component begins to travel through and permeate the organization. As alignment takes place, the energy lifts the known, manages the unknown, and becomes that magical something where the expected and unexpected meet and fully form something much larger and more glorious than the original sum of the individual parts could promise.

The energy behind that alchemy begins when people become clear on who they are, what they do, and how they do it. When dimensionality is added to these understandings, people and organizations begin to normalize, allowing for even greater faith in the future to emerge. Dimensionality creates an opening whereby organizational complexities can be revealed and given some room to breathe. By practicing strategic patience, we see that emergence is a viable option and that we can provide sustenance and allocate resources to growing ideas, strategies, people, and initiatives. We not only see what can be possible, we create an openness to begin to shed what no longer works and is creating blockages and misalignments. Our increased knowing and ability to glimpse at the whole of what can be, fortifies us. Alignment begins to put people in sync with purpose and work is inextricably connected by positivity. The shift is palpable and all involved begin to recognize that their best is encouraged and valued. They understand this because there is an actual definition of their best to guide them. They aspire to and willingly and happily achieve more because they, too, are acting in clarity and can better see how vital they are to the whole of what is happening.

Probably the greatest shift in clarity is an almost natural letting go of fear. We don't talk about this absolute circuit breaker enough in organizations because there is still some outdated understanding that fear is a symptom of weakness instead of a call to action or a cue for reexamination. Properly balanced fear not only motivates me; it is my daily driver. When it goes out of alignment, it is what retards my progress. Still, the word alone unnerves us, and we wonder if our leaders have lost their gumption if they talk of their own fear. Clarity is the magic elixir of fear, both stated and felt.

Clarity allows us to know where we all stand and that we stand in one place together. It enables us to let go of "reserving" something in case we're being cheated or taken advantage of. Clarity pulls back the curtain and reveals the remaining 50 percent of truth, which as we have shared is often untold and almost always unrecognized. It enables us to collectively commit to being all in and to truly rely on and respect one another. A 2014 *Forbes* article, Change Management Requires Leadership Clarity and Alignment, asserts that " ... leaders must have clarity in purpose and focus and an alignment of strategic philosophy and resolution goals. ... There must be a common language that guides execution, monitors progress and allows for course correction along the way. ... Above all, there must be a well thought-out, clearly defined and communicated strategy behind any change management effort—that's where you can begin to show real leadership clarity and alignment." A leader's willingness to fully disclose information in an honest way and foster an inclusive, transparent space for all is the essential foundation which enterprise-wide alignment relies upon.

The alchemy that happens with clarity fans our faith in self and trust in others. In it, we begin to do the real work toward having what we need, when we need it, certain that we can unite together to get us where our vision, dreams, and goals take us. This is about our understanding and willingness to believe that our ultimate performance depends less on our environment and wholly on our understanding of and willingness to embrace the expectations that we or others set for our ultimate success. This great crescendo, created when the expected crashes into the unexpected, causes us to leap forward, beyond what we imagined possible. That's where the magic happens.

THE VALUE OF CLARITY

In clarity, we create new understandings of how change is just a shift in energy, and nothing to fear or back away from. We can't control it or tame it, so it isn't to be labeled a letdown. By being in clarity, we unleash our hold on our desperate desire to resist change, allowing our energy to constantly face forward and be used on what is needed rather than succumbing to circuit breakers that distract and ultimately derail us. Once we learn to ride the waves of change and find purpose and connection in the energy swirling throughout the box, we know and trust that we can break through rather than break apart. We learn that nothing is truly uncertain when we are certain about the important and enduring core of who we are. And, that starts with your definition of your box.

In creation, we know we can kindle a spark that may be flamed, carried on, or adopted by others, maybe even millions of others; over time, we can alter and adapt it until it reaches its ultimate purpose and audience—perhaps one that we couldn't see or even imagine when that first spark ignited. Faced with challenges, we can become absolutely clear about where our contribution can best be made, which will reveal who aligns with our values so that we may partner with them to ensure growth or longevity. Or, maybe we're clear about just enjoying the part of the journey that they share with us, and that is valuable enough.

When and where did we begin to expect that each individual thing was supposed to deliver everything? The universe is made up of particles. So is clarity. Clarity exists as a space in which to serve. It is a dimension within which we can expand influence, elevate results, and optimize all outcomes.

One client, a world-renowned international aviation company with a leading air medical division, embraced the whole of clarity through the process and methodology that you've now learned. When we started working with them, they were a decentralized organization. Each division had the autonomy to do what it wanted, how and when it wanted to. Yet, at the core was an incredible commitment to and shared belief in the company and what they were doing. Our work helped them to become a more purposeful, more focused, and an even more thoughtful organization. Most of all, our work together helped them redefine the ambitious performance metrics, in every area of the company, that they continue to achieve and surpass each year.

When we first started working together, the company operated in an industry faced with negative publicity and challenging safety outcomes. And no matter how safe the company was (they were widely considered to be one of the safest in the industry), they existed in an environment in which it would never be enough. Their original focus on performance and safety had all been based on the value of what happened "during the call," or when lives were being saved in flight. But the truth is, the work they do "before the call" and "after the call," although not as heart-pounding, is just as vital as what happens "during the call." So, an early initiative, with defined operational imperatives and desired outcomes, was developed around the concept of "Beyond the Call." This helped normalize the importance of the role that every person plays, therefore enhancing alignment around every person doing their part for what preceded and followed the "perceived" moments that determined life or death. But, in actuality, it was a group of intentional actions carried out by all, both before and after the call, that made those life-and-death moments "during the call" whole.

As a direct result of the clarity process, they redefined their company and reframed their financial picture from one of loss to abundant success. Now, they are enjoying operational vibrancy and, most importantly, organizational reliability. Clarity helped them see how, as an organization at the forefront of safety, improvements in their safety record could only be actualized by their changes in human behavior, even though dramatic advances in technology already supported safety improvement. More than any other organization we have had the privilege of working with across the world, it was clear to us that nothing mattered more to them than their people. They understood that their extraordinary people were under fire every day—working in an intense emergency environment, an industry that is highly regulated and immensely competitive. Yet, that did not change the expectations of the leadership of the professionals stationed across the globe. They were given the tools, training, and most important, the support necessary to operate at an optimal level at all times.

We learned about the passion of the people in this industry, and specifically this company. Through our travels to their bases and in conversations with their pilots, mechanics, and caregivers, we saw a level of commitment and professionalism that gave us insight into the innermost workings of the workforce and the company itself. We were amazed to learn that even first responders forget how magical the work they do is. To them, the ability to save a life and create a future for someone that would have slipped away without the highly skilled intervention of that responder is simply what they work to achieve each day and "all in a day's work." The leadership understood the psyche of the workforce and knew that simply demanding safety wouldn't incentivize the workers to change behaviors or drive different outcomes.

They wanted to take the progress they had made in the organization and revolutionize how their workers thought about safety, as it is a core value that applies to every second of their day. To get an even deeper understanding, they determined the need to dissect every daily behavior that impacts safety. So, they approached these behaviors by identifying every past action that led to any prior accident, seeking to understand how the mind operates in the process. This helped leadership identify new ways to refine, elevate, and protect their culture to drive safety performance and to ensure that every person would get home safely after every shift.

After conducting a year-long study on the brain and how it functions with repetitive tasks, we collaborated closely with the client to build a one-of-a-kind program that addresses the challenges and barriers that exist within the human brain. The science and design of the program made it automatic—the brain's engagement was *designed* as a critical part of the daily execution. Because the company was already operating in clarity with a highly committed leadership team, alignment and connectivity were already in place to create something revolutionary in the safety space.

Once we developed the foundation of the program, we knew it was important for the program to extend throughout every part of their organization. That way, every person who worked there understood his or her role in creating and operating in safety. Life-Saving Thinking was born. It was the flipside of the company's acclaimed Life-Saving Behaviors effort, for which the company studied every actual cause and contributing factor for every accident in the history of the company. The behavioral study, led by employees, was a painful remembrance of the accidents and the reasons for the loss of life of the men and women who came before them. They learned that there were 10 common behaviors, that, if understood and properly executed, would have prevented each accident. The company's leadership did what few leaders do—they clung to the work and spread it throughout the entire company with a simple message: ALWAYS, which stands for

A

Life-Saving Behavior

Will

Assure

Your

Safety

The message was simple: ALWAYS adhere to each of the 10 behaviors—every person, every time. ALWAYS. But, to the leadership's credit and vision, they also recognized there is always something else to be considered. They understood their box. They were aligned around their purpose, clear with their operations, focused on their engagement, and absolutely committed to their people. When we talk about *change the people or change the people*, this client exemplifies how commitment to what is most important—the people—can forever change the outcome of the organization and save lives in the process. They put tools and education in place to help the people change themselves and support one another. The leadership was steadfast in their belief that good, or even very good, would never be acceptable, because lives were always at stake. They recognized how their conviction to continue investing and believing in human factors would define the future of the company and the safety of their people. Their leadership continued to churn and to invest time, energy, and resources. They knew that there would always be something more.

That is the genesis of Life-Saving Thinking, a program that demonstrated to every employee that the company believed in them and their ability to understand how to use their brain to accomplish what others had not done before. The leaders were determined to understand how the human brain works—but what was most impressive was their absolute determination to get it right—even if that meant delaying the program to do so. They wanted the science to be right. They wanted the design to be right. They wanted the program's launch to be right. They were determined to ensure that every facet was absolutely right, because they knew that if the workforce "got it," it would forever add control to their future. The leaders were convinced that together with Life-Saving Behaviors, Life-Saving Thinking had the potential to be a game changer, and more importantly, a life saver.

Only when it was right was the initiative launched globally—beginning with an innovative, one-of-a-kind, train-the-trainer event for leaders, reminiscent of a high-tech TED talk. It was then subsequently rolled out to each base through a series of carefully crafted, highly creative monthly engagement events and individualized learning modules. Through our assessments and feedback loops with the company, we discovered that the success or failure of this or any initiative depended on the buy-in, understanding, and passion of the base managers.

All of the employees take cues from their managers. At significant expense, the decision was made to include all base managers from across the globe to join the executive leadership team at the offsite launch and education event. No detail was overlooked, from the invitation, to the design of the room and purposefulness of the table setups, to the communications before and after, to the nightly "pillow gifts" and messaging in the attendees' hotel room each evening, to the event itself.

Together, each person shared the experience of an engaging and hands-on introduction, education, and training event. While those convening for the training expected a more traditional PowerPoint presentation, they walked into the space and became immersed in activity and creativity, anchored by a 65- × 25-foot screen as the centerpiece of the room. As everyone got settled in, the room went dark and ambulance sirens immediately started going off and the sound of aircraft taking off filled the room and awakened the senses. The attendees were thrown into purposeful chaos to transport them from where they were to where we wanted and needed them to be. The room changed their orientation, capturing their attention by creating uncertainty and injecting energy. From the get-go, they knew something was going on and that the experience was going to be different from what they had expected.

Inevitably, they could grasp that what happened at that introduction mattered. It was a big deal. They had all been brought together to experience something significant—not just being talked to or presented at—but fully engaged in every sense. They were not simply told that multitasking was not acceptable, they were shown why with creative interpretations of games from our childhood, like tic-tac-toe and Simon Says. In each case, the leader was challenged playing the simple games, but a twist was incorporated with math problems and memory exercises layered on. Hands-on activities and interactive exercises reinforced the message. The room transported them. The activities changed them. The people part of it created energy and alchemy to bring the elements together and create magic.

Magic is more than innovation. Innovation alone is not enough because it engages only the mind. Once something moves into experience, it is adopted and experienced in a more complete way. At Deutser, we talk about how magic is the convergence of the expected with the unexpected. The hard work of creating the space of clarity, aligned with the goals, dreams, and purpose of an organization, produces palpable energy and forward propulsion that combine into something more glorious than the individual parts could ever equal. It is the transformation that happens within people that make these efforts both take hold and explode with possibility and viability, joined as one. In clarity, you share with others in a way they can experience the dimensionality of something they may have never considered before.

Back to our story. The results were extraordinary. By bringing leaders from around the world together to immerse them in discussions and activities that challenged their minds and taught them how to leverage the power of their brains to improve safety performance, the company made a statement to the entire industry about its commitment to understanding and improving human factors. We understood that if we can change the experienced mind of a leader, then we have a real chance to change the mind of every professional in the organization. While traditional policies and safety practices provide structure and guidelines on how to work safely, this concept of Life-Saving Thinking offers a memorable, innovative, and unique lens. From this viewpoint, the employee can really understand how his or her own brain works and utilize it—recognizing mind traps that exist, making decisions, and completing tasks with the individual's full and complete attention.

In fact, we recognized that traditional safety policies can represent two classic masqueraders: best practice and policy. Knowing this, it was critical that we identify ways to pull the mask off of these typical programs and bring safety to an even higher level at this organization. This program is changing minds, reducing risk, and saving lives. If saving lives isn't magical enough, the president of the company saw the profound impact of Life Saving Thinking and felt compelled to share it and make it available to competitors in the industry at no cost. He taught us, and continues to remind us every day, that safety will never be a point of competition among us. It is something that we, as leaders, have a responsibility to share. The groundbreaking importance of Life-Saving Thinking was recognized by receiving the industry's Vision Zero Safety Award. The award, accompanied by a cash prize, allowed this life-saving effort to be shared and implemented inside other companies across the industry, with its possible adoption as an industry standard. Now, that's magic.

This is how clarity fills and expands your box. Once you undergo the process to achieve clarity, you'll see a connections are being made, behaviors clearly communicated, and the vibrancy of your organization becoming a power grid of clear purpose and shared commitment. With that, the entire organization and everyone you reach is energized and lit up.

Clarity empowers people in extraordinary ways. It fosters confidence and deep understanding. Unexpected outcomes change your thinking. It sets a new standard. Clarity can both normalize and propel you forward at the same time.

Clarity doesn't depend on one solution, linear thinking, or absolutes. It allows you to generate magic inside of a six-sided box in which you can see all the elements and choose the levers to activate, making an impact of your choosing. Then that reveals something else that informs you. Inside your box, you can normalize, sustain, grow, and move forward, all while knowing who you are, what you do, and why you do it. It is the magic of your own ability to control that construction that both protects and nourishes and becomes that which withstands and even thrives in chaos, change, and uncertainty. If you think of the sides of that box as being permeable rather than fixed, it frees the flow of input information in and the release of old ways and toxic byproducts out and away from your core.

Life-Saving Thinking and other impactful initiatives launched and developed with our clients not only create magical effects at work, elevating people and ideas; these principles begin to change lives *outside* of work. We create an environment where, in clarity, change is embraced instead of feared. As a leader, you have elevated not only your performance and bottom line, you have elevated *people*. This is more rare than you think—and when you do make that connection and move the people forward, your company is forever changed. And, I promise you that nothing else feels quite as magical as when people who entrust their careers to you become engaged, elevated, optimistic, and excited. After all, isn't that why we became leaders?

While thinking about what makes great leaders who lead with clarity, I want to tell you about another client, whom I consider a tremendous generator of lasting impact through his contribution of creating other leaders. This leader of a nationally recognized, top-ranked entrepreneurial program was also fascinated by the brain, specifically in reference to how the best entrepreneurs think. He was determined to create a program that goes beyond the traditional education of entrepreneurs in teaching them all the right tools and topics they need to acquire the necessary knowledge, along with the practical aspects of understanding business plans, profit-and-loss statements, budgets, and so on. He was inspired to really zero in on what makes an entrepreneur excel and elevate not only the business they lead, but themselves and other people. That was his clarity conundrum, and he wanted to be in clarity about how to build a model program that would train entrepreneurs in an entirely different and sustainable way. He wanted to build an educational platform that helped them create a successful business, but more importantly, a successful life.

Traditional business education relies on teaching the hard tools and skills needed to become an effective businessperson, but the leadership of this program found that there was a human quality that may be a greater predictor of entrepreneurial success. They wanted to create a firm foundation by connecting entrepreneurs with an intense and insightful knowledge of who they are and why they want to become entrepreneurs. Besides their business dreams and goals, their life goals are integrated and elevated through the program. Clarity was constructed around this belief and commitment to life in business, which integrates both the head *and* the heart. This began to inform the way in which they recruit, select, and engage their students. An entrepreneur must continuously create and fiercely lead the vision of the organization while inspiring people to share in his or her vision and ultimately taking it beyond what he or she originally dreamed possible.

Our client decided to build an entrepreneurial program that combined both hard and soft skills, one that would gracefully combine the mind and heart in the making of entrepreneurial excellence. Most faculty aren't given the time to address the perceived "soft stuff," but this college embraced the soft stuff as the glue that connected the leader to his or her ultimate success. It was not optional; it was embedded from the first day they entered the program and infused every day until they graduated. These students are taught using the essentials of the Deutser method and each construct their own six-sided box, which is updated and examined throughout the program each semester—connecting having a dream to the act of having a plan. The program ingrains a deep understanding of their dream—something that can easily become lost in academia altogether. Students are asked: Why do you want to be a CEO? Why do you think that a particular thing is important? They start with what they want, then what they have to do to effectively get what they want. Students are provided with business simulations that include elements of chaos, ambiguity, uncertainty, and change. They are exposed to the concept of transition in diverse scenarios before they must navigate it in real-life situations, where their investment and dreams are at stake. Ultimately, they learn who they want to be and what kind of business they want to have and how their actions will not only make them successful, but sustain them for years to come.

With clarity, remember, comes magic. So we weren't at all surprised to see that they have an abundance of alumni participation—from entrepreneurs who have been trained in the same way, by cultivating both the head and the heart. Because of the successful entrepreneurs' transformation in the past, they now feel compelled to return the favor. So, they become mentors to current students and recent graduates, provide connections, and generate resources that will help to support and expand a broader community of entrepreneurs with clear values and plans. The entrepreneurs in this leading program, ranked in the top five across the country year after year, challenge their entrepreneurial students by asking, "How does your business becomes sustainable?" All of the graduates and students know the core values of the program as well as their own, and can articulate them. More than that, they live them as great leaders do. They are taught not what to think, but how to think in a way that can be applied to all business conundrums.

Using the principles and methodology of being in clarity, they learn not just how to operate a business but how to move in the world so that they can more readily see the connections that their business makes and identify and amplify the points of contact. They now have a process to look at themselves, through any change, either internal or external, and readily connect with their values, dreams, vision, and goals. Failure in this program is perceived to be when a student comes through the program and fails to connect with who he or she really is and they leave unchanged. The idea of pretending to be someone you are not is not connecting the heart and the mind, and certainly can't exist in clarity. Any student who doesn't light up and engage would be discouraging to this educational leader. But, 100 percent of their previous four years of entrepreneurial students said it changed their lives—perhaps in part because of these strategies in which they construct their space of clarity and update it at given points throughout each semester. They learn the process. This education provides not only confidence to run their business, but confidence to run their lives. That is truly advanced education.

The process that develops clarity can be taught and replicated to extend through your organization. It empowers the easy transference of values, culture, and ideals. For every system made whole, it deepens dimensionality, constantly crafting the space and clarity within, giving you a perpetual backup plan and an ever-expanding reality of probabilities. I have a clear picture of who I am and how I am creating value. It is no small feat to constantly carry forward a reverent knowledge of who you are and what is enduring about what you do, along with what you provide that no one else can quite satisfy. Your reputation is who people think you are, your character is who you are, and when those are aligned, you have the ability to become successful.

In clarity, this becomes how you think and act. Clarity creates success in life—hand in hand with success in business. Clarity has a broad reach. As we observe and study business failures, more often than not, we see that they centered around the person at the head of the organization. He or she had not examined the process of leading. They had not added value to when and how what they do better than anyone else would travel up and down and throughout the organization. They did not understand their box and their own relation to it.

Leadership style is characterized by many traits. A lifestyle leader or entrepreneur is often very different from a tech entrepreneur, but who you are and how you take on problems with grit and persistence will ultimately tell your story of success or failure. Each success and failure won't be your final destination; it will be a point on your clarity map that elevates you to your next magical moments, extending your reach. Operating in clarity creates an environment in which *people* become the heart of everything.

When they become the heart and soul of everything, lives are changed—both those who work for the organization, and those who are touched by its work and outreach. This was especially true when we were hired by a financially strapped healthcare system that played a major role in a mid-sized market. This system, which was acquired by a larger institution, was given an abrupt 90 days to turn their business around. And by business, they meant everything. We were basically brought in to save the day. Everything was stacked against us and certainly stacked against them. They even wanted to pay us the bulk of our fees after the 90 days. My CFO was not excited by the gamble, but our team was energized by knowing what was at stake for them, for us, and for the thousands of men and women who worked across the system. This was way bigger than us and we knew it. But most important, there were thousands of patients who would be affected by our success or failure. We knew that we had to quickly address the core tenets of the process that you have followed throughout this book.

But here, we knew that one thing could quickly unite all and that was the deep caring of what could happen to these patients. It seems obvious that, like education is about the student, health-care is about the patient. Unfortunately, as we have seen, this is not always the case—there are times where it is about something or someone different. It may be the physician, the nurse, or the leader. But, in this case, the research was clear. And so was the directive. Put the patient in the center—not with words, but with real, meaningful, and measurable expectations.

We started our effort with two letters: *CE*—Clinical Excellence. There was so much negativity swirling around the health system, and rumor and innuendo ruled the narrative. We held true to a belief I have always carried with me—simplicity is power. We needed to bring that concept together in a way that people could see it, feel it, and understand it. And, they could remember it and put it into their daily actions. We wanted to lift everyone out of the panic of the 90-day decree and their worry about the what-ifs that dictated their mood and ruled the pervasive current state of mind.

The system needed to unite around the one thing that mattered to everyone. People. The strategy focused on the people. The culture exercise focused on the people. The outreach and education focused on the people. The financial conversations always went back to the people. The biggest shift was the care and concern focused on the people. The dialog was less about the business of the business, and more about the business of people. Everyone rallied around the idea that if the system failed, then they would all fail. Suddenly, the competitive spirit they had used against each other was now used to propel the system forward. Unused buildings were set for demolition to save money. Underperforming assets were mobilized in different ways. Leadership that was misaligned with the board's vision and expectation was reassigned or changed out. Processes were rethought and new pathways of working were reimagined. The highly strategic CFO navigated the system through challenging business arrangements, and like a judo master, leveraged them to strengthen the system as opposed to working against it. The highest-performing asset was also rethought and repurposed to increase the likelihood of success of a historically underperforming flagship location. The vision was clear. The expectation was clear. The expected behavior was clear. So too, was the changing identity becoming clear. Every aspect of their box was clear. But the one thing that was missing was the collective belief in and positivity that the future could be different from the past. Much like the entrepreneurial program and the aviation story you read earlier in the chapter, the belief system—the heart of the system—had to be addressed, understood, and changed before anything else could be elevated.

Although we launched numerous initiatives at once, the one that is most remembered for bringing the system, and more importantly, the people, together in clarity was an interactive event and whole system planning exercise. More than 7,000 people inside and outside the system were figuratively transported to the future. While people want and need hope, they rarely have the ability to see the future, much less experience it. Simply put, it is often challenging for the workforce, focused on their day-to-day responsibilities, to see a different vision—that is, the role and expertise of a leader. For a system in a desperate financial situation, the idea of hosting an interactive, futuristic event seemed a little outlandish and irresponsible. But the visionary CFO understood that if the people could not see, or more importantly experience the future, they could not ever get to the destination. So he encouraged the development of an experience that would become transformative. And it was.

People were formally invited to a Disney-like experience in which every detail was considered, from the communications before, during, and after; to the messaging; the activities; the environment; the sensations; and emotions—no touchpoint was left unconsidered. Everything was purposeful and everything was built with the box in mind. People entered the space through a tunnel highlighted with lights, sounds, and inspiring "positivity-focused" graffiti. They then watched an instructional video that told them they were about to be transported to the future—before entering the actual event space that used lights, technology, sounds, and highly designed graphics and oversized glass walls with word searches and other games to inject a sense of purposeful fun. Every 10 minutes of the experience, a new video message encircled the room, followed by a period of socialization of the message and normalization of the reality it presented. Each person was then tasked with contributing strategic insights and direction though a series of exercises and prompted questions as part of the journey to CE. In this whole system planning exercise, each person in the system was required to fill out oversized translucent sticky notes at stations around the room and then paste them on glass walls—sharing personal stories of success, stating and committing to the one change they would make to create the greatest positive impact on the success of the system, reorienting their minds around positivity—their own and their health systems'. It wasn't simply about transformation—it was about transporting the minds, hearts, souls, and bodies of each person connected, regardless of how, around the new vision and strategy. It became a push-and-pull experience inside the organization and outside the organization. And, as the expectations changed, so did the results.

Magic happened every day that week when the experience was open. A community of physicians, caregivers, administrators, board members, community leaders and supporters, media allies, and even some competitors, as well as philanthropists alike were transported by possibility and aligned through CE. The agreement was clear that they all valued and needed to deliver the most excellent care they could. The well-trained staff, though affected by many chaotic and uncertain factors, knew that they wanted to be a part of providing clinical excellence—something that no one before them in the system had delivered.

We all want to be part of greatness and history. Magic happened when the vision of what could be and the shared value of clinical excellence converged and created magic. That experience gave people hope and gave the system life. There have been other strategies since the box was first introduced, but that experience forever changed the future, while the system remains aligned, profitable, high-functioning, and healthy. And most of all, focused on the clinical excellence it strived to provide.

Clarity enables us to lead while being whole—individually, as an organization, and then extending it to customers, clients, patients, vendors, fans, supporters, members, and all who experience us. In clarity, there is depth and dimension that provides a richness in experience centered around a core that brings along with you the tools, people, and energy needed to nourish and sustain your endeavors.

Magic is the convergence of all that we've talked about. And, when magic does happen, we are able to achieve a measure of impact that is beyond our wildest expectations.

CONCLUSION: DECODING YOUR CONUNDRUM

We each are faced with our own unique conundrums. Sometimes they are ignored. Sometimes they dominate our mind space. And, yet other times, they are a pervasive presence that is simply an ongoing irritant. One thing is clear, they impact our organizations and each of us, as leaders, differently. But, there is a universal antidote that empowers leaders to decode their conundrum and lead in clarity.

In that spirit, I want to share this final exercise with you that we use to help others experience clarity. It is purposely designed with a spirit of fun as well as a measure of thoughtfulness and creativity. As you work to unravel your conundrum and build your box, enjoy where the game takes you.

As a wise man once shared with me as I first entered the work world, life is a never-ending road. He explained that there will be places to speed up and slow down, places to turn right and left, as well as opportunities to explore new paths. He urged me to never question the decisions I made and to keep looking inward and striving forward. But most importantly, he reminded, you have to first get on the road and always lead with clarity.

★CLARITY★CODE★

HOW TO PLAY
Roll the dice and end up with an accidental plan for your company's future. Or, begin at Start and take the steps outlined below to experience better performance achieved in Clarity.

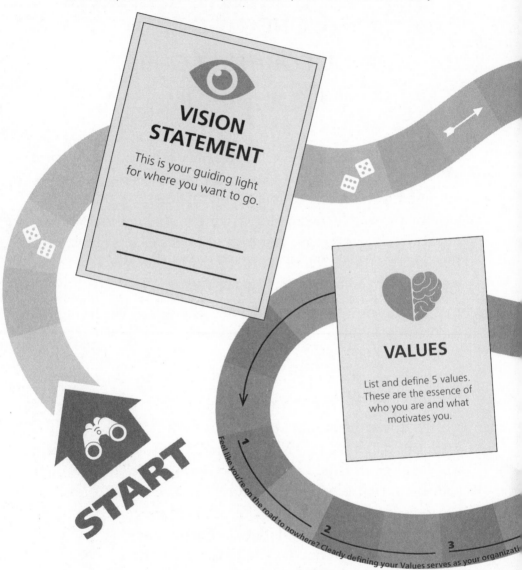

VISION STATEMENT
This is your guiding light for where you want to go.

_____

_____

VALUES
List and define 5 values. These are the essence of who you are and what motivates you.

Feel like you're on the road to nowhere? Clearly defining your Values serves as your organizati

1

2

3

These are actions/behaviors that demonstrate your
imperatives, and vision; what it looks like in daily life. C
are fundamental and exhibited by the entire organiza
Leadership behaviors are specific to mana
List 5 for each and develop examples to b

START

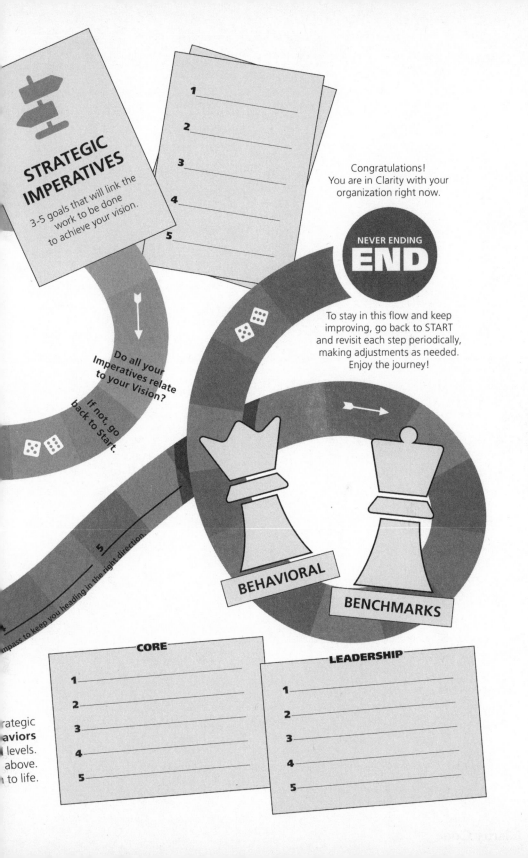

STRATEGIC IMPERATIVES

3-5 goals that will link the work to be done to achieve your vision.

1 _____
2 _____
3 _____
4 _____
5 _____

Congratulations!
You are in Clarity with your organization right now.

NEVER ENDING
END

To stay in this flow and keep improving, go back to START and revisit each step periodically, making adjustments as needed. Enjoy the journey!

Do all your Imperatives relate to your Vision?

If not, go back to Start.

...mpass to keep you heading in the right direction.

5

BEHAVIORAL

BENCHMARKS

rategic
aviors
levels.
above.
to life.

CORE

1 _____
2 _____
3 _____
4 _____
5 _____

LEADERSHIP

1 _____
2 _____
3 _____
4 _____
5 _____

ACKNOWLEDGMENTS

Being able to share my life's work and that of my team is one of my great professional and personal honors. We have spent decades studying, implementing, and creating clarity for and with some of the most incredible, visionary, and honorable leaders, men and women whose names you may not know, but whose commitment and extraordinary work have undoubtedly touched you at some point. We owe our success to them, the people who trusted, who believed, who understood that clarity could change their future and that of their companies.

While we strive to be in clarity in all parts of our lives, for me, clarity starts at home with my family, who are my inspiration, my love, and my life. Jill, thank you for your encouragement, support, unwavering love, and steadfast belief in me always and forever and ever. You have been by my side in every journey—sharing, encouraging, prodding, and always loving. You pushed clarity before I knew that clarity existed. You are clarity personified in how you live your life and treat others—you are the greatest gift and blessing in my life. And, to the most wonderful and special gifts in my life, Ashley and Andrew. You are the most precious angels that light my world and feed my soul. Your intellect and piercing wisdom have propelled my thinking and your unwavering love for me fuels me in everything I do. You are the most kind, creative, talented people in my life, and you drive me to excel every day in life and love. I love you all more than anything in the world. My family is my love, my everything, my clarity.

Mom and Dad, you gave me creativity, helped write my papers, design my reports, read my books, showed me that every detail matters, demonstrated that there is no day off, and taught me that with work ethic I can accomplish anything. You taught core values long before they were in the mainstream. You defined the box from which I have operated. I love you more than you know, and am forever grateful for the clarity and love you have brought to my life. Debbie and Steven, no person could love their brother and sister as much as I love you. You were my first and best friends, you were my first confidants and my first believers. We have an unbreakable bond and form one of the great support systems anywhere. And, Sarah, my other sister, you have brought such love and creativity to our family, and your mandalas have brought great trajectory and clarity to our office. My grandparents—immigrants, entrepreneurs, community leaders—set an indelible example of what it means to love, to give, to work hard, to overcome, and to succeed in business and in life. Frann, thanks for picking me and sticking by me, and us, no matter what. Jeff's and your presence is always with us and your strength gives us clarity. Martha and Harris, thanks for your kindness and gentle reminder about the good guys. Your never-ending belief in finding a cure, lending a hand, and changing the world is inspiring. Jason, thanks for your unwavering belief in me, for your friendship and brotherhood, and for being by my side in every journey. Todd, I am grateful for all we have and continue to share together. Michael, Wayne, Adam, Jon, Marc, what can I say—no matter the moment, you have always been there, believing when no one else knew what to believe. And, to Patrick, Britt, Jeff, Jean-Pierre, Mike, and Jan for your sharing and believing. You epitomize what it means to be great dads and leaders. And, to the men and women of YPO Gulf States for sharing values, a passion for entrepreneurship and a belief in doing business the right and humble way.

Leading Clarity is a dream brought to life through the passion of the most intelligent, committed, creative, and brilliant people that I get to work with every day. They are the real inspiration behind what we do and how we change companies. They could do anything anywhere, but they choose to help leaders, to change companies, to save lives, to make magic happen. They challenge thinking, constantly innovate, and drive for clarity in all we do. Peter, you have been the great thinker, creator, and voice in how to transform companies and people. Alan, your brilliance, your work ethic, your visionary strategic abilities are unparalleled, so, too, is your friendship. Peter and Alan, no one has impacted more leaders than you with your unwavering commitment and piercing clarity. Diane, your brilliant creative mind and uplifting spirit, and positive energy drive and inspire me and everyone that your magical work and kind heart touches. Adam, thanks for saying yes and making this happen on every level, for showing me that numbers are cool, for being the one to put words into action and making them work, and for providing balance in all we do. Molly, thanks for your unrelenting encouragement, honest feedback, courage to be you in every situation, wise counsel, and enduring friendship; Coert, for your conviction in doing what is right, always, and your willingness to do what real friends do, tell the truth at all times; Diana, thank you for your absolute friendship, constant advice, patience, leadership, and making sure I get through each and every day with clarity of mind and spirit; Linden for challenging every thought, providing wise counsel and a steady hand, and making great things happen; Hayden for your energy, passion, deep thinking, and unbelievable way with words; Catherine for your daily sacrifice and daily drive to make this a better world; Michelle, Mary Jean, Jill, and Jennifer for your ability to take napkin notes and create masterpieces; and Lydia, Grace, Kristine, Ashleigh, Gregg, Kelly, Santiago, Katie, Karen, Jill, Abby, Katy, Ms. Lorraine, and everyone else for all you add each and every day to bring clarity to others. Our work is our work because of you.

I will never find the proper way to thank Nancy Hancock, my collaborator, my voice and my dear friend, who challenged thinking, pushed us to dig deeper, and gave life and meaning to this book. Her words create magic, touch the soul, and change minds. I am forever grateful to her for expanding my thinking and sharing my voice. Most of all, I am looking forward to the clarity we will continue to deliver together and the lives we will impact. Thanks to Shawn Achor for being the inspiration for what it means to change lives and performance through positivity. This all started with your moving words and your introduction to Jordan Brock, who has been at my side, providing encouragement and advice. And, thanks to my agent, Greg Ray, whose constant support, wise counsel, and big thinking have given me comfort and direction. Thanks to Shannon and the publishing team at Wiley. I sincerely appreciate your guidance and genuine belief in this book. And, to the special people who have shown me how to not only take care of myself, but prepare myself to take care of others—Johnnie Mae, Helen, Magdalena, Josh, Wendi, Richard, Judy, and Erica.

While my life's work is helping leaders find clarity, it is actually they who have shared their clarity with me. These are the true leaders in our society. They are men and women of extraordinary character and purpose. They exude goodness in their personal and professional lives and I am honored to have been by their side in some small way as they have led their teams to extraordinary heights. Dave, you inspire and humble me every single day with your brilliance, dedication, unwavering trust, and more, your moral compass. I learn from you and am driven to excel because of your leadership and friendship. Barry, your intellect, wisdom, and generosity of spirit and counsel have no bounds. You are the reason I am in business. Tom, your leadership in crisis and steady hand every day ground me and provide comfort. Lance, your gentle spirit and committed manner create indebted followers. John, you believed in what we do before there was something to believe in. Al, you have taught me how to lead through crisis with unusual calm and unwavering determination. Dave, you allowed us to help define and create the next generation of entrepreneurs by connecting their minds and their hearts. Cesar, you shared your vision and entrusted us to make magic with you, changing the lives of hundreds of thousands of people along the way. Cindy, you captivate me with your stories, your strength, and your gift of leadership. Neil, thank you for allowing me to be part of your family and the amazing work you lead. Andy, your willingness to lead from the front and always do what is right, regardless of the consequence, is a blessing to me and everyone you impact every day. Steve, your careful hand, piercing intellect, and trusting way have allowed so many to be impacted across the region. Priscilla, you showed me to dream big and see the world through my own eyes. Britt, you took a chance when you didn't have to, entrusting your business and your future to us. Kelly, thank you for allowing us to be part of the magical change you create everywhere you go. Kevin, you inspire with your brilliance and big ideas. Mike, your vision for what can be is only paralleled by your incredible work ethic. Bob and Gina, thank you for your never-ending vision of what can be for our region and for having the strength to make it real. Brad, thank you for sharing your careful leadership, thoughtful words, and genuine concern for the wellbeing of others. Blair, thank you for the leadership roles you have given me and model you have provided. David and Amalia, thank you for leading, and believing in second chances. Larry, you showed me the power of new ideas on a daily basis.

Carol and Cici, you gave me a chance and stood by me. You showed me that belief in one's vision is all one needs and you allowed me to explore to the far reaches of my box. Gary, thanks for showing me courage and the warmth of your genuine heart in the face of life's great adversity. David, thank you for letting go of the past and believing in growth and second chances. TJ and Tim, you have shown me that it is not where you start, but how hard you work to overcome any obstacle in the way. Sydney, you welcomed me in when no one else would talk to me—giving me hope and opportunity, even if it was the circus. Todd, you challenged me, taught me, and changed me. Fred and John, what better partners could one have—you gave me the space to create, no matter how crazy the creation was. Bert, you were the role model who taught me to never slide with my legs up, to say no to hard candy, to erase the invisible wall between men and women, and to always do what is right. You were there clapping when the world was silent. You showed me to never talk about values, but live them. Bernie and all the Greylockers along the way, you are the boys that defined my early life and gave me the direction and belief that I could be anyone or anything I ever dreamed. Cyvia, your strength of purpose and character inspire and move me. Melvyn, you gave me my first chance in business. Your lessons will always stay with me and your spirit will always be embodied in our work and our way of working.

Each of you are a blessing. I would not be who I am or be able to do what I do without you. You have each brought something that has become part of me. I thank you for being who you are and for sharing it with me, and countless others. I genuinely believe that the clarity that you share is a reflection of the clarity of your soul. Thank you for the inspiration and light that you provide on this magical journey. Because of you, I remain in clarity.

About the Author

Brad Deutser is a thought-provoking counselor and trusted confidant to leaders in diverse industries around the world. He brings a unique, highly creative approach to problem solving and to changing futures for leaders and their companies.

As a business advisor, culture authority, creative strategist, and executive coach to CEOs, board chairs, and top corporate management for high-profile organizations—including Fortune 500 companies and leading nonprofits—Brad leverages his unique perspective and pedigree to drive organizational performance. As President and CEO of Deutser, he is the visionary behind this innovative consulting firm focused on helping organizations and their leaders achieve clarity to drive business performance, as well as Deutser Clarity Institute, a think-tank, idea accelerator, and innovative learning lab.

Brad's insight and approach to organizational clarity has transformed many prominent organizations, including those in energy, education, healthcare, industrial services, private equity, professional services, retail, and cause-based industries. His perspective on leading with clarity is central to his success working with leaders in transition and crisis. He has worked with and for many high-profile organizations, helping them navigate chaos, effect change, and drive performance.

He is committed to effecting change at a societal level and has infused socially responsible and cause-related principles in not only his clients' practices, but his own firm's as well. The Deutser Clarity Fund was created to support causes that bring clarity to the community and help people in need. He has also created individualized micro-funds for each employee so they can personally impact organizations of importance to them. Additionally, Brad serves in leadership and board chair capacities for numerous organizations in education, healthcare, and not-for-profit institutions, including the Gulf States Chapter in Young Presidents' Organization.

After graduation from the University of Texas with an Economics degree, he worked for several companies, including the London-based solicitors firm, Blackburn Gittings & Nott; the nation's leading socially responsible marketing company, Cone Communications in Boston, MA; as well as Ringling Bros. and Barnum & Bailey Circus and Walt Disney World on Ice. Brad is a frequent speaker on issues of clarity. He has been a guest lecturer at universities, conferences, and at corporate events across the country. He is passionate about helping young people achieve clarity and leverage their talents to the fullest.

Brad's clarity comes from his deep relationship with his family, including his wife of more than 20 years and two loving children, who are the light of his life.

REFERENCES

Allen, M. S., & McCarthy, P. J. (2016). "Be Happy in Your Work: The Role of Positive Psychology in Working with Change and Performance." *Journal of Change Management*, *16*(1), 55–74.

Babatunde, B. O., & Adebisi, A. O. (2012). "Strategic Environmental Scanning and Organization Performance in a Competitive Business Environment: Economic Insights." *Trends & Challenges*, *64*(1), 24–34.

Boss, Jeff (2017). "How to Turn Office Ambiguity into Organizational Clarity." *Forbes*, https://www.forbes.com/sites/jeffboss/2017/02/22/how-to-turn-office-ambiguity-into-organizational-clarity/#1ee5181958e0

Frisch, Bob (2012). "Culture vs. Strategy Is a False Choice." *Fast Company*, https://www.fastcompany.com/1817137/culture-vs-strategy-false-choice

Harvard Business Review (2016). "How Employee Alignment Boosts the Bottom Line." https://hbr.org/resources/pdfs/comm/betterworks/19764_HBR_Reports_BetterWorks_May2016.pdf

Hay Group (2012). "Sustaining Culture Change: True Culture Transformation Requires More than a Cosmetic Corporate Make-over: How Can Companies Re-align Culture and Make Change Stick?" http://www.haygroup.com/downloads/uk/culture_transformation_viewpoint_2012.pdf

Llopis, Glenn (2014). "Change Management Requires Leadership Clarity and Alignment." *Forbes*, https://www.forbes.com/sites/glennllopis/2014/06/30/change-management-requires-leadership-clarity-and-alignment/#3b75859b3e3c

Rothwell, William J. (2011). "Why Organizations Use Competencies." ATD Newsletter, https://www.td.org/Publications/Newsletters/Links/2011/07/Why-Organizations-Use-Competencies

Schwartz, Howard S. (2013). "Reality and Truth in the Politically Correct Organization: The Case of the Dan Rather Memo Debacle at CBS News" (January 26, 2013). https://ssrn.com/abstract=2207369 or http://dx.doi.org/10.2139/ssrn.2207369

Trevor, J. & Varcoe, B. (2017). "How Aligned Is Your Organization?" *Harvard Business Review*, https://hbr.org/2017/02/how-aligned-is-your-organization

Ursrey, Lawton (2014). "Why Design Thinking Should Be at the Core of Your Business Strategy Development." *Forbes*, https://www.forbes.com/sites/lawtonursrey/2014/06/04/14-design-thinking-esque-tips-some-approaches-to-problem-solving-work-better-than-others/#73b60cbf1627